KV-408-551

Practice Papers for SQA Exams

Standard Grade   General | Credit

Modern Studies

Text © 2010 Jayne Ashley, David Fyfe and Ruth Sharp
Design and layout © 2010 Leckie & Leckie

01/150510

ISBN 978-1-84372-774-3

Published by Leckie & Leckie
An imprint of HarperCollins*Publishers*
Westerhill Road, Bishopbriggs, Glasgow, G64 2QT
T: 0870 460 7662   F: 0870 787 1720
enquiries@leckieandleckie.co.uk   www.leckieandleckie.co.uk

A CIP Catalogue record for this book is available from the British Library.

Questions and answers in this book do not emanate from SQA. All of our entirely new and original Practice Papers have been written by experienced authors working directly for the publisher.

Leckie & Leckie makes every effort to ensure that all paper used in its books is made from wood pulp obtained from well-managed forests, controlled sources and recycled wood or fibre.

Leckie & Leckie would like to thank the following for permission to reproduce their copyright material: as indicated in book

Special thanks:
From Ruth Sharp to Guch Dhillon and Jane West for their advice and support.
From Jayne Ashley to her Mum, for shining light in the darkness and for quite simply, always being there.
From David Fyfe to Mary, for support and putting up with me.

Introduction

Layout of the Book

This book contains exam advice and practice exam papers which mirror the actual SQA exam as much as possible. The layout, paper colour and question level are all similar to the actual exam. This will help you to become familiar with what the exam paper will look like.

The answer section is at the back of the book. Each answer is similar to that which would be included in the markers' guidelines. The answers also include practical tips on how to tackle certain types of questions, some details of how marks are awarded and advice on just what the examiners will be looking for.

You should start by reading this introductory section.

How to Use This Book

The Practice Papers can be used in two main ways:

1. You can complete entire practice papers as preparation for the final exam. You could complete the practice papers under exam style conditions by setting yourself a time for each paper and answering it without using any references or notes. Alternatively, you can answer the questions as a revision exercise, using your notes to produce a model answer. You can then use the answering sections to check your work.

2. You can use the Topic Index at the start of this book to find questions within the book that deal with specific topics or particular types of questions. This allows you to focus on areas that you particularly want to revise or, if you are mid-way through your course, you can use the index to select and revise the areas you have already covered in class.

The Exam

Question 1 – Living in a Democracy

The Government, your representatives, elections in the UK, pressure groups and trade unions.

Question 2 – Changing Society

The elderly, families, employment and unemployment.

Question 3 – Ideologies: USA or China

Rights and responsibilities, participation in politics, economics, immigration/migration and inequalities in the USA or China.

Question 4 – International Relations

Politics of aid in Africa, security interests and threats, the European Union (EU), United Nations (UN) and North Atlantic Treaty Organisation (NATO).

In these practice papers and in the SQA exam there is a **choice in Question 3**. You will have studied either The USA or China. You will not have covered both in your Standard Grade course. Do not answer both areas or you will run out of time in the exam.

In Standard Grade Modern Studies there are seven key concepts. You will need to show knowledge and understanding of these concepts in your answers.

Concepts	Exam Area	Description
Representation	Q1	How elected representatives, like MSPs, act on our behalf.
Participation	Q1 and 3	To take part in society. Voting is a common form of participation.
Rights and responsibilities	Q1 and 3	The freedoms you have. The need to take your freedoms seriously, e.g. using your right to vote.
Ideology	Q2 and 3	The political and economic ideas used to run a country.
Equality	Q2 and 3	This often focuses on inequality. Why some groups are worse off than others.
Need	Q2 and 4	The problems some people in the UK have and how these are tackled. The problems that many people in developing countries have and how these can be tackled.
Power	Q4	The power that some countries and organisations have over other countries.

General Level

- You have 90 minutes for this level.

- This works out at about 22½ minutes for all parts of each question area.

- Allow a few minutes to read each question thoroughly.

- Make sure you know exactly what the question is asking you to do.

- There are 28 marks allocated for KU questions and 36 marks for ES questions.

Credit Level

- You have 120 minutes for this level.

- This works out at about 30 minutes for all parts of each question area.

- Allow a few minutes to read each question thoroughly.

- Make sure you know exactly what the question is asking you to do.

- There are 32 marks allocated for KU questions and 40 marks for ES questions.

Other Useful Advice

KU and ES

You should already know that KU stands for Knowledge and Understanding and that ES stands for Enquiry Skills.

Extra Knowledge

Most of the ES questions in this book will add to your knowledge. Unless otherwise stated, in the answer section, the sources are factual and the information can be used in KU answers.

KU mark allocation

KU questions are worth four, six, eight and ten marks. Some well developed points may be awarded up to three marks. However as a general rule aim to write two detailed points for a four mark, three detailed points for a six mark and four detailed points for an eight-mark question.

ES questions

Other than the Investigation set of questions you should **not** use your own knowledge in ES answers. You will know the investigating set by the picture of the man with a question mark in his head.

Read each question thoroughly before you begin to answer it – make sure you know exactly what the question is asking you to do.

For longer answers, like the **Credit 8 mark question**, you could plan your answer by making a few notes or doing a quick mind map. This would allow you to check at the end that you have covered all the main points.

Don't repeat yourself as you will not get any more marks for saying the same thing twice.

USA and China

This is often highlighted by the SQA as a weaker section for you. You must use specific information relating to the country you have studied.

Revision Advice

Work out a revision timetable for each week's work in advance – remember to cover all of your subjects and to leave time for homework. Make sure that you have some time off to relax. This gives your brain a chance to process all the information. Try to start studying early in the evening when you are still more alert.

Arrange your study time into one hour or 30 minutes sessions, with a break between sessions of 15 minutes. Do something different during your breaks like having a drink or listening to music. Remember to stick to your break timings.

Everyone revises differently, so find the way that works for you. Some people work best on their own while others work better with a partner. If you are working with someone you could try marking each other's answers.

Mobile phones and MP3 players can be used to record your revision notes. You could use this book and your class notes to make up mind maps on the various topics that you have studied.

You could start a checklist of key words and their meanings like the example started below.

Elections – Keywords	Meanings
Candidate	Someone standing for election
Election Agent	Someone appointed by the candidate to run the election campaign
Canvassing	To contact people door to door or on the telephone to try to persuade them to vote for your party.
Manifesto	A list of the policy promises made by each political party.

ES Question Types

ES Questions	Meaning/Explanation
Differences – General only	Explain why two sources are different. You must quote one point from one source and then the disagreeing point from the other. You should then repeat the process once more for a four mark question.
Exaggeration – General only	This means that there is something wrong with the view or the statement of the named person. You have to state clearly which parts of the view are wrong and provide evidence to prove it.
Conclusions	There will be bullet points telling you what to make conclusions about. You should write one clear conclusion for each bullet point. Then give evidence to support the conclusion. Repeat the process to cover all bullet points. At Credit you will have to make well developed points and provide comparisons within and between the sources.

Support **or** disagree at General only Support **and** oppose at Credit and General	Again you will have a view or statement from a person. At General you may be asked to give two reasons to support **or** to disagree with the view. You will need to identify and quote the correct parts of the statement to support **or** disagree with. You will then have to show why you support **or** disagree using the evidence from the sources. At Credit level, and in some General questions, part of the view will be correct and the other part will be wrong. You need to state clearly which is which and prove it using the evidence.
Option choice/ decision making	You will get two projects or two people and you will have to pick one. You need to be able to explain your choice clearly. At Credit you will be asked to say why you rejected the other option. There is no right or wrong answer; it is how you use the evidence that matters.
Selective in the use of facts – Credit only	This is slightly like a support and oppose question. From the view or statement you need to identify what is selective and what is not selective, in the use of facts. Selective points will be wrong. Points that are not selective will be true. You need to state clearly which is which and prove it using the evidence. You must provide an overall conclusion or conclusions on how selective the view or statement is.
Investigation set (hypothesis – Credit only)	**Hypothesis:** (Credit only) Your hypothesis must be relevant to, and show understanding of, the issue. A hypothesis is statement which can be proved or disproved. It should never be in the form of a question. **Aims:** Your aims must be relevant to your hypothesis (Credit)/topic (General). Aims are what you would need to find out to complete your investigation. **Enquiry methods questions:** You may be asked to state and justify investigation methods. You could be asked to explain the advantages or disadvantages of a given method. You could be given a method, e.g. a webpage and be asked to comment on it. You must know and understand the different methods of enquiry and their limits. **Methods include:** Interviews, internet, surveys/questionnaires, letter, emails, libraries, newspapers, databases and observational visits.
In some KU questions you will see the following terms:	
Explain	Provide a detailed description of a point. Remember you should **always** give an example for every point you make.
Describe	Provide a reason **why** something is the way it is. Your point should be explained **in detail**. Remember you should **always** give an example for every point you make.

Good luck!

Topic Index

Practice Papers for SQA Exams: Standard Grade General/Credit Modern Studies

Topic – Knowledge and Understanding	General Exam A	General Exam B	Credit Exam A	Credit Exam B	Knowledge for Prelim			Knowledge for SQA Exam		
					Have difficulty	Still needs work	OK	Have difficulty	Still needs work	OK
Question 1 – Living in a democracy										
Trade Unions	1a			1a						
MPs representing their constituents		1a								
Rights of pressure groups	1c	1c		1b						
Local Councillors			1a							
Rights and responsibilities in a democracy			1b							
Question 2 – Changing Society										
Meeting the needs of the unemployed	2a		2a							
Why some people have difficulty getting a job	2b									
Needs of elderly		2a		2a						
Why some elderly are healthier than others		2c								
Question 3 – Ideologies USA (A) or China (B)										
Why some people are better off than others	3(B)a	3(A)a								
Social and economic inequalities	3(B)c 3(A)c			3(B)a						
How citizens participate in politics	3(A)a	3(B)a	3(B)a	3(B)a						

Topic – Knowledge and Understanding	General Exam A	General Exam B	Credit Exam A	Credit Exam B	Knowledge for Prelim			Knowledge for SQA Exam		
					Have difficulty	Still needs work	OK	Have difficulty	Still needs work	OK
Question 4 – International Relations										
European Union	4c		4a							
The United Nations				4a						
NATO	4c	4a								
Needs in African countries	4a		4b							
Why give aid to Africa		4c								

Enquiry Skills Index	General Exam A	General Exam B	Credit Exam A	Credit Exam B	Knowledge for Prelim			Knowledge for SQA Exam		
					Have difficulty	Still needs work	OK	Have difficulty	Still needs work	OK
Exaggerations (General only)	3d, 4d	2b, 4b								
Differences (General only)	1b	2d								
Support and/or Oppose/disagree	2c, 2d, 3b	1b, 3b	3b	2b						
Conclusions	4b	1d	4b	2c						
Option Choice/Decision Making		4d	1c	3b						
Selective in the use of facts (Credit only)			3c	1c						
Investigation set (hypothesis at Credit only)	1c, d, e	3c, d, e	2b, c, d, e	4a, b, c, d						

General Level Exam A

Modern Studies

Standard Grade: General Level

Practice Papers
For SQA Exams

General Level
Exam A

1. You have 1 hour 30 minutes to complete the exam.

2. Try to answer all of the questions in the time allowed.

3. For Question 3 you should only answer ONE section:

Either Section A – The USA
Or Section B – China

Scotland's leading educational publishers

SYLLABUS AREA 1—LIVING IN A DEMOCRACY

QUESTION 1

> Trade Union Members can take many different actions during a dispute.

(a) Describe **two** actions that a member of a Trade union can take during a dispute aimed to increase pay.

4 marks, Knowledge and Understanding

(b) Examine the following sources then answer the question below.

SOURCE 1

View of Patricia Kerr

The 2007 election was the third election to the Scottish Parliament since the referendum was held in 1997.

Voter turnout was the lowest it had ever been for a Scottish Parliament election with only 52% of people voting. We need to encourage more people to use their vote.

There was no difference in the voter turnout in each of the 8 Parliamentary regions. At least more than half of the electorate turned out to vote in all the regions.

There are nearly 4 million people eligible to vote in Scotland which means that they can take part in elections for the Scottish Parliament.

SOURCE 2

View of Eric Richard

Scotland has a population of 6 million people; 4 million of whom are entitled to vote in elections for the Scottish Parliament.

It is not necessary to take any action about encouraging more people to vote. Voter turnout was low but not as low as it had been in 2003 when it was 49%. The highest turnout for an election in Scotland was 58% in the 1999 election.

The 2007 Scottish Parliament election was the third election held since the Scottish Parliament was created in 1999.

Voter turnout varied quite significantly across the Parliamentary regions. For example, in the West of Scotland region 56.8% turned out to vote whereas in the Glasgow region only 43.2% people voted.

The sources give views about participation in elections for the Scottish Parliament.

Give **two** differences between these views.

In your answer, you can only use the information in the sources above.

4 marks, Enquiry Skills

QUESTION 1 (CONTINUED)

 You are investigating the following topic:

> *WOMEN IN THE SCOTTISH PARLIAMENT*

(c) Give **two** appropriate aims for your investigation, as part of the planning stage.

2 marks, Enquiry Skills

(d) You decide to contact a female MSP from each of the main political parties.

Give **two** different ways in which you could contact the female MSPs you have chosen.

Explain why each way you have chosen is a good way to get information for your investigation.

4 marks, Enquiry Skills

You use the Internet to help with your investigation.

(e) Describe **one** way in which you could use the Internet in your investigation.

2 marks, Enquiry Skills

SYLLABUS AREA 2—CHANGING SOCIETY

QUESTION 2

> The Government tries to help young unemployed people to find jobs.

(*a*) Describe **two** methods that the Government uses to help young people find jobs.

4 marks, Knowledge and Understanding

> Some groups find it more difficult to find a job than others.

(*b*) Select **one** of the following groups:

- Older Workers
- Single Parents

Give **two** reasons why the group you have chosen may have difficulties in finding a job.

4 marks, Knowledge and Understanding

QUESTION 2 (CONTINUED)

(c)

Levenside Health Authority and local council to invest in new health programme

The health and wellbeing of those living in areas of deprivation within the Levenside Authority is set to be improved. The programme is seeking to target the increasing numbers of unemployed people who smoke and fail to take regular exercise. There are several areas of deprivation within the Health Authority that suffer high levels of unemployment and poor housing, which are known to contribute to poor health.

<table>
<tr><th>PROGRAMME A</th><th>PROGRAMME B</th></tr>
</table>

Community Development	**Healthy Lifestyles**
People living within Levenside will benefit from money invested by the Health Authority and local council.	The money invested by the Health Authority and local council will be used to encourage those within Levenside to follow more healthy lifestyles.
Local companies will improve the quality of housing of the poorest areas within the Health Authority by providing central heating and new windows.	NHS nurses will be employed to distribute information and help smokers give up their habit with special mobile counselling clinics. It is planned to concentrate on areas of high unemployment.
Improvements to the playing fields and parks in deprived areas will provide free leisure facilities to give the unemployed and those on low incomes more opportunities to take regular exercise.	A team of fitness experts will also be employed to offer free evening training sessions at a range of local schools in deprived areas.
This community development programme will help to improve the health of all those living within Levenside.	Following a healthier lifestyle will improve the health of all those living within Levenside.

Read through the information above and decide which programme (**Programme A** or **Programme B**) would be the better choice for Levenside Health Authority to meet the needs of unemployed people living within that area.

Give **two** reasons that support your choice of Programme.

In your answer you must link the information about the needs of the affected group of people to the programme you selected.

4 marks, Enquiry Skills

QUESTION 2 (CONTINUED)

(*d*) Examine the following table then answer the question below.

	Elderly Survey – Most Needed Services		
	2005	**2007**	**2009**
Free Health Care	29·2%	25·6%	23·1%
Cheap Travel	16·5%	18·0%	19·2%
Heating Allowance	22·7%	24·1%	24·8%
Meals on Wheels	10·2%	9·8%	10·4%
Faster NHS Appointments	12·9%	13·6%	11·7%
Flu Vaccinations	6·0%	6·4%	9·1%
Other	2·5%	2·5%	1·7%

Of the elderly people surveyed, free health care has always been seen as the most important service that they needed. Between 2007 and 2009 the service with the biggest rise in importance was meals on wheels.

View of Graham Black

Read the 'View of Graham Black' then **give two reasons to disagree** with this view.

In your answer, you can only use the information in the table above.

4 marks, Enquiry Skills

SYLLABUS AREA 3—IDEOLOGIES

Important!

Answer **one** section only: Section (A) USA (Pages 16 to 18)

                        OR   Section (B) China (Pages 19 to 21)

QUESTION 3

(A) USA

(*a*)

> American people can influence the government through interest groups.

Describe **two ways** that American people can influence the government through interest groups.

You must use American examples in your answer.

4 marks, Knowledge and Understanding

(*b*) Examine the following sources then answer the question below.

SOURCE 1

Information About Selected US States		
State	**Gun Ownership Rate (per 100,000)**	**Gun Death Rate (per 100,000)**
Colorado	30	11·5
Arizona	38	18·1
Montana	52	14·5
Oregon	43	10·5
California	14	9·8

SOURCE 2

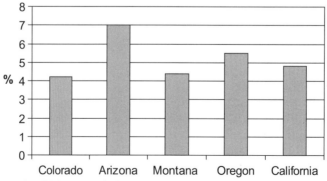

Unemployment Rate by State %

Adapted from www.statemaster.com/graph/cri_mur_wit_fir-death-rate-per-100-000, http://newsbatch.com/gc-regionowndeath.html, CDC&swivel.com, www.statemaster.com/graph/eco_une_rat-economy-unemployment-rate

QUESTION 3 (A) (CONTINUED)

> The state of Montana has the lowest unemployment rate of most other selected states. However the citizens of Montana have both the highest rate of gun ownership and gun deaths.

View of Mary Wardrop

Read the 'View of Mary Wardrop' then give **one** reason to support and **one** reason to oppose this view.

In your answer, you can only use the information in the sources above.

4 marks, Enquiry Skills

(c)

> Some American people are more affected by crime than others.

Give **two reasons** why some American people are more affected by crime than others.

You **must** use American examples in your answer.

4 marks, Knowledge and Understanding

QUESTION 3 (A) (CONTINUED)

(d) Examine the following sources then answer the question below.

SOURCE 1

The economic crisis has caused many problems for countries throughout the world and the banking system has been blamed for the credit crunch. An estimated 1.5 trillion dollars has been provided by the government to restore the USA's failing financial system. Several countries have taken strong action to support the banks and to try to control the amount of bonuses that are paid to employees. President Obama has taken a range of strong measures that will limit the size of large banks so that their collapse would not put the financial system and world economy in danger.

SOURCE 2

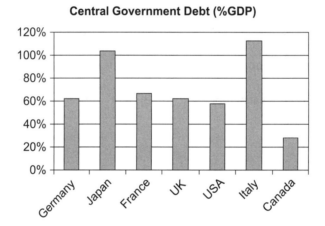

Central Government Debt (%GDP)

The credit crunch has caused huge problems in the USA and the banks are generally to blame. President Obama has done nothing to control how these banks operate. The government has spent huge amounts of money to help the banking system but our level of debt in the USA is higher than most other rich countries and we cannot afford to spend taxpayers' money in this way.

View of Pamela Harrington

Read the 'View of Pamela Harrington'.

Write down **two** statements made by Pamela Harrington which are exaggerated.

Then give **one** reason why each of the statements you have chosen is exaggerated.

In your answer, you can only use the information in the sources above.

4 marks, Enquiry Skills

QUESTION 3 (CONTINUED)

(B) CHINA

(*a*)

> Some people in China are better off than others.

Describe **two** reasons why some people in China are better off than others.

You must use Chinese examples in your answer.

4 marks, Knowledge and Understanding

(*b*) Examine the following sources then answer the question below.

SOURCE 1

The views of people in selected areas on how serious a threat they think global warming is.

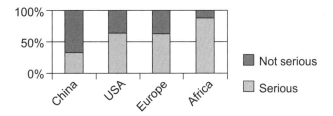

Adapted from – http://news.bbc.co.uk/1/hi/sci/tech/8345343.stm

NB the data is actually sourced from Gallup poll data taken in 2008. Between 528 and 2,493 people interviewed in each country, either by phone or face-to-face (the question was put to people who said they knew something about climate change). The margin of error ranges from +/−3·5 to +/−5·3%.

SOURCE 2

Chinese President Hu Jintao has promised to greatly reduce Chinese CO_2 emissions by the year 2020. CO_2 is one of the main gases causing global warming.

Currently 70% of the energy supplies in China come from coal power stations. This form of power creates high levels of CO_2 emissions. President Hu has said that China hopes to reduce the use of coal and increase the amount of power from cleaner sources including hydro (water), wind and solar power in the future.

As China has become wealthier, the country has been using more energy. Many people in China are still poor and they want to have the same lifestyle as the better off Chinese. This means that the demands on energy will continue to increase.

Adapted from – http://news.bbc.co.uk/1/hi/sci/tech/8268792.stm

QUESTION 3 (B) (CONTINUED)

> Chinese people do not take global warming as seriously as people in other parts of the world. The Chinese already get most of their energy from cleaner sources like water, wind and solar power.

View of Yang Jinping

Read the 'View of Yang Jinping' then give **one** reason to support and **one** reason to oppose this view.

In your answer, you can only use the information in the sources above.

4 marks, Enquiry Skills

(c)

> Social inequalities exist in China.

Describe **two** social inequalities that exist in China.

You must use Chinese examples.

4 marks, Knowledge and Understanding

QUESTION 3 (B) (CONTINUED)

(d) Examine the following two sources then answer the question below.

SOURCE 1

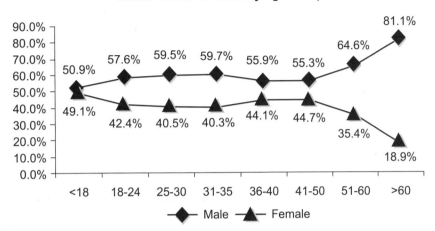

Gender Online in China by Age Group

http://www.seomoz.org/blog/china-ten-things-you-should-know-about-an-online-superpower

SOURCE 2

Camps for Internet Addicts

Some teenagers in China have become so addicted to using the internet that they have been sent, by their parents, to special camps to try to break their addiction.

The people who run these camps describe an internet addict as anyone who is on the internet for at least six hours a day and has little interest in school.

The camps treat the teenagers with a programme of early rises, physical exercise, medication and counselling.

Many people are unhappy about these camps because some teenagers have been beaten. One teenager died as a result of their injuries.

Adapted from – http://news.bbc.co.uk/1/hi/world/asia-pacific/8219768.stm

---

Males in China are more likely to go online to use the internet than females. Men aged 36–40 are more likely to go online than any other group. In China there are special camps to help treat young people who are addicted to the Internet. Everyone is very happy about the work of these camps.

View of Allison Black

Read the 'View of Allison Black'.

Write down **two** statements made by Allison Black which are exaggerated.

Then give **one** reason why each of the statements you have chosen is exaggerated.

In your answer, you can only use the information in the sources above.

4 marks, Enquiry Skills

SYLLABUS AREA 4—INTERNATIONAL RELATIONS

QUESTION 4

(a)

Promoting peace	Health Care	Education

Choose **one** of the issues above.

Describe how improvements in your chosen issue would help meet the **needs** of people in some African countries.

4 marks, Knowledge and Understanding

(b) Examine the information in the table then answer the question below.

UNAIDS 2008 HIV/AIDS figures in selected African Countries

Country	Overall % of population aged 15–49 years with HIV/AIDS	% in towns/cities with HIV/AIDS	% in countryside with HIV/AIDS
Ethiopia	2%	5·5%	0·7%
Kenya	7·7%	10·0%	5·6%
Malawi	11·9%	17·1%	10·8%
Uganda	5·4%	10·1%	5·7%
Zambia	15·2%	23·1%	10·8%
Zimbabwe	15·3%	17·0%	15·0%

(Information from – http://apps.who.int/globalatlas/predefinedReports/EFS2008/short/EFSCountryProfiles2008_MW.pdf & http://www.unaids.org/en/CountryResponses/Countries/default.asp)

Write **one** conclusion for each of the following:

• The country with the highest overall rate of HIV/AIDS.

• The difference between HIV/AIDS rates in towns/cities compared to the countryside.

Give evidence for each of your conclusions.

In your answer, you can only use the information in the table above.

4 marks, Enquiry Skills

QUESTION 4 (CONTINUED)

(c)

> NATO and the EU both play a beneficial military role.

Give **two** ways in which either the membership of NATO or the development of the military role of the EU is of benefit to the UK.

4 marks, Knowledge and Understanding

(d) Examine the timeline then answer the question below.

Date of Joining the EU	Total Membership	EU Member Countries
1958	6 countries	Belgium, France, (West) Germany, Italy, Luxembourg, Netherlands
1973	9 countries	Denmark, Ireland, UK
1981	10 countries	Greece
1986	12 countries	Portugal, Spain
1995	15 countries	Austria, Finland, Sweden
2004	25 countries	Cyprus, Czech Republic, Estonia, Hungary, Latvia, Lithuania, Malta, Poland, Slovakia, Slovenia
2007	27 countries	Romania, Bulgaria
2011		Currently Croatia, Macedonia and Turkey are hoping to join the EU in 2011

> There are currently 27 member countries of the European Union (EU). The United Kingdom became a member of the EU in 1973. In the last ten years very few countries have joined the EU. No other countries are now interested in joining the EU.

View of Grace Wilson

Read the 'View of Grace Wilson'.

First, write down **two** statements made by Grace Wilson which are exaggerated.

Then give **one** reason why each of the statements you have chosen is exaggerated.

In your answer, you can only use the information in the timeline above.

4 marks, Enquiry Skills

[End of Question Paper]

Credit Level Exam A

Modern Studies

Standard Grade: Credit Level

Practice Papers
For SQA Exams

Credit Level
Exam A

1. You have 2 hours to complete the exam.

2. Try to answer all of the questions in the time allowed.

3. For Question 3 you should only answer **one** section:

Either Section A – The USA
Or Section B – China

SYLLABUS AREA 1—LIVING IN A DEMOCRACY

QUESTION 1

(a)

> Local Councillors represent their constituents in many ways.

Fully explain how local councillors can **represent** their constituents.

4 marks, Knowledge and Understanding

(b)

> In a democracy people have many rights and responsibilities.

Fully explain the **rights and responsibilities** people have in a democracy.

4 marks, Knowledge and Understanding

(c) Examine the Background Information about Dunbarrie Textile factory and Sources 1 and 2.

BACKGROUND INFORMATION

- The Dunbarrie textile factory is situated in the village of Lockhart in the North East of Scotland and has been the main employer in the surrounding area for over 60 years. This is a rural area with a population of over 60,000 people. Lockhart suffers from the same fate as many other rural communities; young people are forced to move to towns and cities to find work.

- The factory has made textiles for companies abroad and across the UK. The textiles have been used for many different functions including designer handbags, specialist furniture and womens' clothes. There are 2,000 employees in the factory.

Contract	Female	Male
Part-time*	426	55
Full time**	208	1213
Temporary*	98	0

*Receive some holiday pay but no pension entitlement
**Entitled to holiday pay and company contributions to pension plan

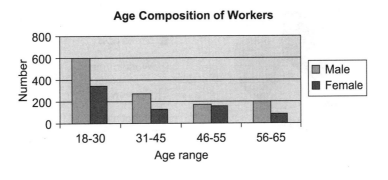

Age Composition of Workers

QUESTION 1 (CONTINUED)

- Dunbarrie textile factory offers a good place of employment for young people, particularly school leavers, as it provides an 'in-house' training service that leads to them achieving qualifications, ensuring good promotion and employment prospects in the company.

- Up until recently the company has enjoyed a healthy business and, in fact, in 2005 even took on extra staff as they were receiving so many orders from abroad. However, the recent economic downturn and the recession across the UK has led to a substantial drop in orders. This has led to the company being forced to look at redundancies as a way of saving money and keeping the business from collapsing. So far a total of 284 employees have taken up the offer of voluntary redundancy. However the company are now considering the option of making more staff redundant through compulsory redundancies; the number of staff they are considering making redundant could be as much as 500 which would be a major blow to the local economy. In a recent staff survey, 56% of employees stated that job protection should the main priority for the new Shop Steward, only 16% of workers said that improving pension rights and increasing holiday entitlement was a priority at this time.

- Most workers in the factory are members of the Trade Union, UTWS. While the Trade Union and Management of the factory enjoy a good relationship now, this has not always been the case. Twelve years ago workers took strike action over holiday entitlement and the management responded harshly. The staff eventually went back to work having achieved nothing. There is much debate between employees about the course of action the Union should take in this current dispute over redundancies.

Survey of Staff Attitudes

What is the most important quality in a Shop Steward?

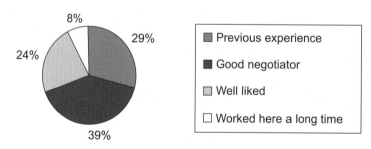

■ Previous experience
■ Good negotiator
▨ Well liked
☐ Worked here a long time

What is the best course of action to take to prevent further redundancies?

▨ Strike only as a last resort
■ Strike now
▨ Work to rule
☐ Go slow
■ Negotiate

QUESTION 1 (CONTINUED)

There are two people hoping to be elected to the job of Shop Steward to represent people in the Dunbarrie textile factory. Here are summaries of information about them.

SOURCE 1

Information About Margaret Paterson

- Margaret has worked at the Dunbarrie textile factory since she left school 20 years ago. She is well known and well liked by her colleagues.

- Margaret believes that Trade Unions should focus on two main priorities: 1) to safeguard existing jobs and prevent further redundancies and, 2) to improve the pension rights of workers.

- She thinks that the best way to improve pay and working conditions of the workforce is to negotiate with management. She believes that strikes should only be used as a last resort and only after every other action has been taken.

- Although Margaret has no experience of being a Shop Steward, she has experience of negotiating with management to bring about an improvement in working conditions when she was part of the staff committee. This committee was successful in introducing more flexible working hours.

- One of her main areas of interest is looking at the rights and working conditions of part-time and female workers; particularly holiday pay and pension rights. As someone who has been affected by this in her working life, Margaret believes that she is best placed to represent this group of workers.

SOURCE 2

Information About Hugh Robinson

- Hugh thinks that the situation over voluntary redundancies has become so serious that the workforce should be out on strike and that no other action open to them will be successful.

- He believes that Trade Unions are vital for their members, not just to improve pay and protect them from redundancies but also to improve the quality of staff training and improve the health and safety environment for the workforce.

- One of Hugh's main concerns is the prospect for young people in the industry. Hugh would like to see the company investing money for improved staff training. He would also like to see an improvement in the rights of part-time workers; in relation to improving pension entitlement and holiday pay.

- Hugh has some experience of negotiating with management. When he was Shop Steward at his last job he successfully negotiated a new pay agreement for all staff at the factory.

- Hugh has worked in Dunbarrie textiles for a few months. He has previously worked in a similar factory where he was Shop Steward for four years.

QUESTION 1 (CONTINUED)

    (i)   State which person would be more suitable to **represent the workers** of Dunbarrie textile factory.

    (ii)   Give **three** detailed reasons for your choice.

    (iii)   Give **two** detailed reasons why you rejected the other candidate.

You must relate information about the Dunbarrie textile factory to the information about the two candidates for the Shop Steward position.

In your answer, you can only use the information in the background information and the sources above.

10 marks, Enquiry Skills

SYLLABUS AREA 2—CHANGING SOCIETY

QUESTION 2

(a)

> The government helps to meet the needs of the unemployed.

Fully explain how the government tries to meet the **needs** of the unemployed.

8 marks, Knowledge and Understanding

 You are investigating the following topic:

> **Elderly people and residential homes**

(b) State an appropriate hypothesis.

2 marks, Enquiry Skills

(c) Give **two** aims/headings that will help you to prove or disprove your hypothesis.

2 marks, Enquiry Skills

(d) You interview some elderly people in a residential home.

Describe **one** advantage and **one** disadvantage of interviewing some elderly people in a residential home.

4 marks, Enquiry Skills

QUESTION 2 (CONTINUED)

You use the internet to collect more information for your investigation and find this site:

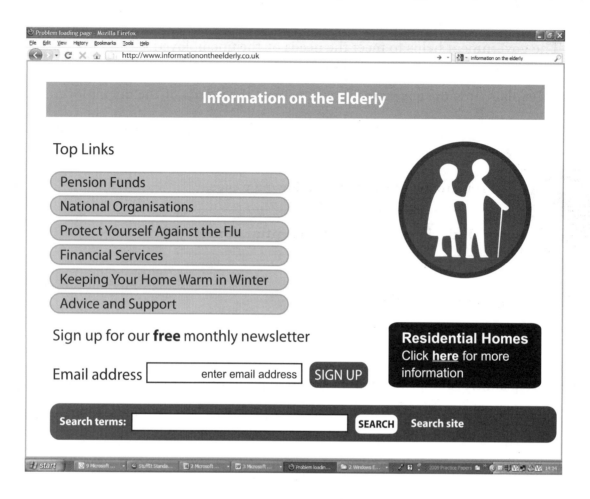

(e) How would you use this site? Explain your answer.

2 marks, Enquiry Skills

SYLLABUS AREA 3—IDEOLOGIES

Answer **one** section only: Section (A) USA (Pages 33 to 36)

                    OR   Section (B) China (Pages 37 to 40)

QUESTION 3

(A) THE USA

(a)

> *Some ethnic minority citizens are beginning to participate more in politics in the USA, whilst others continue not to.*

Fully explain the reasons why some ethnic minority citizens are beginning to **participate** more in politics in the USA, whilst others continue not to.

You must use American examples in your answer.

8 marks, Knowledge and Understanding

(b) Examine the following two sources then answer the question on the following page.

SOURCE 1

Voter Turnout by State (%)			
	2000	**2004**	**2008**
New Jersey	50%	56%	60%
Oregon	60%	68%	63%
North Carolina	41%	52%	63%
California	45%	48%	50%
Nevada	41%	50%	50%
Arizona	41%	50%	49%
Maine	67%	73%	72%
Washington	57%	62%	62%
Florida	48%	58%	60%
Vermont	64%	65%	67%

QUESTION 3 (A) (CONTINUED)

SOURCE 2

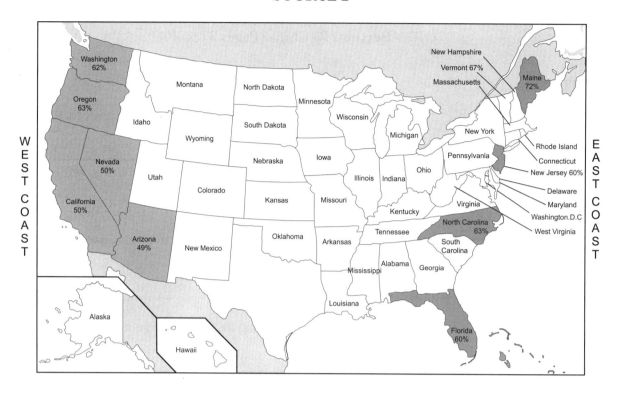

The highest voter turnout figures in 2008 are all to be found in the East Coast states. The largest increase in voter turnout between 2000 and 2008 has been in North Carolina.

View of Julie Smith

Read the 'View of Julie Smith'.

Give **one** reason to support and **one** reason to oppose this view.

In your answer, you can only use the information in the sources above.

4 marks, Enquiry Skills

QUESTION 3 (A) (CONTINUED)

(c) Examine the following 3 sources then answer the question below.

SOURCE 1

The Death Penalty Reporter

In 2005, Kenneth Lee Boyd made history in a North Carolina prison by becoming the 1,000th person to be executed in the USA since the Supreme Court re-instated capital punishment in 1976. This event led to increased debate over the use of the death penalty in the USA.

There is now clear evidence of a shift in both public and official opinion. A survey last month showed that 64% of Americans still favoured the death penalty.

However, this the lowest level of public support in 27 years, down from a high of 80% in 1994. When respondents were offered life without parole as an alternative punishment, more choose life without parole (48%) than the death penalty (47%).

The costs of Capital punishment can be very high. In Texas, a death penalty case costs an average of $2·3 million, about three times the cost of imprisoning someone in a single cell at the highest security level for 40 years.

Sources based upon http://www.deathpenaltyinfo.org/documents/FactSheet.pdf

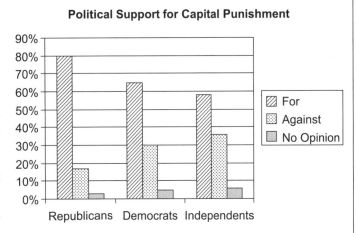

Political Support for Capital Punishment

For / Against / No Opinion — Republicans, Democrats, Independents

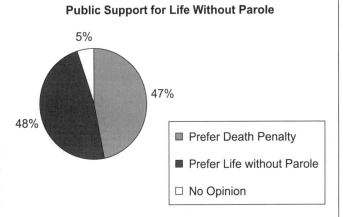

Public Support for Life Without Parole

5% 47% 48%

Prefer Death Penalty
Prefer Life without Parole
No Opinion

Arguments for Capital Punishment

- Capital punishment permanently prevents the worst criminals in our society from committing further crimes.

- It offers real justice to victims' families by providing effective retribution.

- It saves money because not having to pay for long prison sentences saves tax payers' money.

- It deters criminals from committing terrible crimes.

Arguments against Capital Punishment

- Innocent people have been executed in the past and capital punishment means this mistake can never be corrected.

- Executing a human being is brutal and reduces the value of human life.

- Innocent family members of the criminal have the ordeal of living through their loved one's execution.

- The costs of legal expenses before executions can take place are huge.

QUESTION 3 (A) (CONTINUED)

SOURCE 2

In a national poll released in 2009, the nation's police chiefs ranked the death penalty last in their priorities for effective crime reduction. The officers did not believe the death penalty acted as a deterrent to murder, and they rated it as one of most inefficient uses of taxpayer dollars in fighting crime.

Criminology experts were against capital punishment and agreed that the death penalty does not reduce the number of murders and rejected the notion that the death penalty acts as a deterrent to murder.

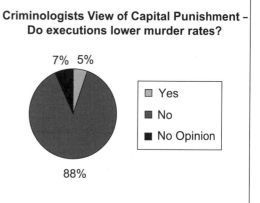

Criminologists View of Capital Punishment – Do executions lower murder rates?

7% 5%

- Yes
- No
- No Opinion

88%

SOURCE 3

The 2008 FBI Uniform Crime Report showed that the South had the highest murder rate. The South accounts for over 80% of executions. The Northeast, which has less than 1% of all executions, again had the lowest murder rate.

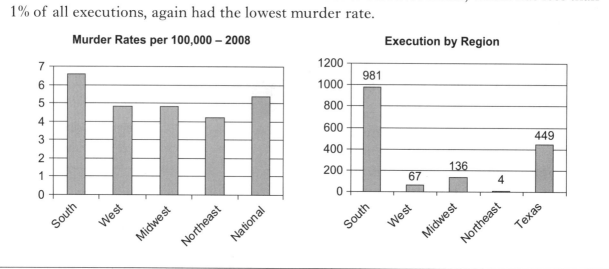

Murder Rates per 100,000 – 2008

Execution by Region

The death penalty is not an effective punishment to reduce the murder rate in the USA and its use is opposed by all groups within the USA. There are no arguments in support capital punishment.

View of Alan Hunter

Read the 'View of Alan Hunter'.

Fully explain the extent to which Alan Hunter could be accused of being selective in the use of facts.

In your answer, you can only use the information in the background information and the sources above.

8 marks, Enquiry Skills

QUESTION 3 (CONTINUED)

(B) CHINA

(a) | Some political rights are limited in China.

Fully explain how political rights can be limited in China.

You must use Chinese examples in your answer.

8 marks, Knowledge and Understanding

(b) Examine the two sources then answer the question below.

SOURCE 1

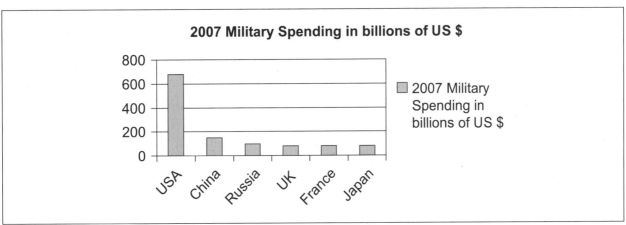

2007 Military Spending in billions of US $

- 2007 Military Spending in billions of US $

USA China Russia UK France Japan

Based upon http://yglesias.thinkprogress.org/archives/tag/defense-budget

SOURCE 2

Over the next decade, China's military spending is expected to increase while U.S. military spending is expected to decline. Chinese military spending is expected to reach $200 billion a year by 2020.

China is also changing military priorities with an overall reduction in military manpower and more spending on building and purchasing advanced weapons and improving information technology. It is spending heavily on advanced fighter jets, computer-guided missiles, satellite-navigation systems and various other high-tech military equipment.

Based upon http://factsanddetails.com/china.php?itemid=294&catid=8&subcatid=51

China spends far less money than the US on its military. The military priorities of China have not changed in the last twenty years.

View of Andrew Morrison

Read the 'View of Andrew Morrison'.

Give **one** reason to support and **one** reason to oppose this view.

In your answer, you can only use the information in the sources above.

4 marks, Enquiry Skills

QUESTION 3 (B) (CONTINUED)

(c) Examine the three sources then answer the question below.

SOURCE 1

The Death Penalty in China

In China the idea behind the death penalty is that it is the best way to deter other people from committing the same crimes. It is not just violent offenders that are punished with death in China. Credit card fraud, tax fraud, corruption and drug-related crimes can get the death penalty in China. There are more than 60 offences, in China, for which a criminal can be executed.

Some offences, including drug-trafficking, carry a compulsory death sentence. China's death penalty has several exemptions for people under the age of 18 years of age at the time the crime was committed and pregnant women. Also under Chinese law people suffering from mental health disorders should not be held responsible for their actions.

In 2005 a top government official was put to death for taking bribes. This reminded people that criminals may face death for less serious crimes.

The country is believed to execute more people than anywhere else in the world, with 1,718 executed in 2008, according to Amnesty International (the actual number of executions is a state secret). However by Amnesty International figures Iran and Saudi Arabia execute more **people per head of population**.

Written source adapted from http://www.teachabroadchina.com/china-death-penalty-capital-punishment/ and http://www.guardian.co.uk/world/2009/jul/29/china-death-penalty-executions

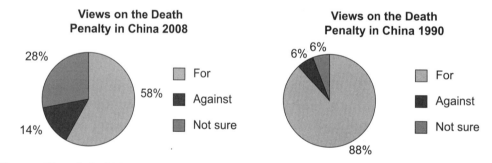

Views on the Death Penalty in China 2008
28%
58%
14%
For
Against
Not sure

Views on the Death Penalty in China 1990
6% 6%
88%
For
Against
Not sure

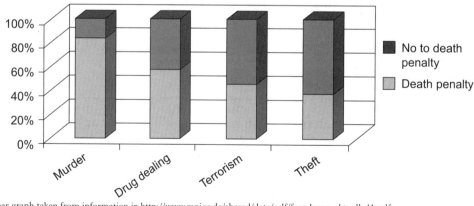

Views of People in China About the Use of the Death Penalty for Different Types of Criminal

Murder   Drug dealing   Terrorism   Theft

No to death penalty
Death penalty

Pie chart & bar graph taken from information in http://www.mpicc.de/shared/data/pdf/forschung_aktuell_41.pdf

QUESTION 3 (B) (CONTINUED)

SOURCE 2

Most Chinese people accept the death penalty and it looks unlikely that it will be abolished any time soon. However the Chinese government does plan to reduce the number of people it executes.

The Chinese Supreme People's Court (SPC) monitors executions and now has the right to overturn death sentences handed down by lower courts. The China Daily said the SPC overturned 15% of death sentences handed down in 2007 and 10% of those issued in 2008. Some experts think that this change has caused a drop in executions of as much as 30% but with no official figures it is difficult to tell.

Zhang Jun, vice-president of the SPC, said that the death penalty should be applied to "an extremely small number" of very serious offenders.

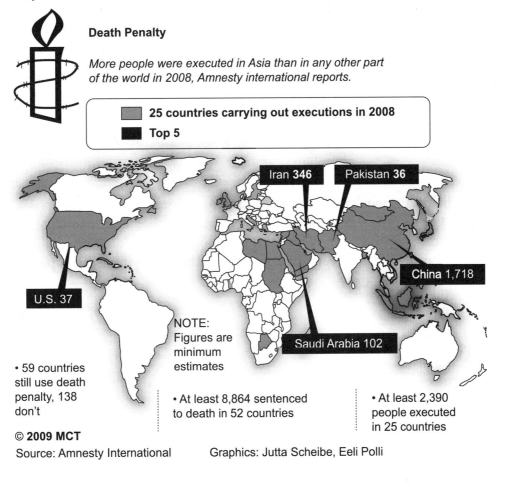

Death Penalty

More people were executed in Asia than in any other part of the world in 2008, Amnesty international reports.

| | 25 countries carrying out executions in 2008 |
| | Top 5 |

Iran 346   Pakistan 36

U.S. 37

China 1,718

Saudi Arabia 102

NOTE:
Figures are minimum estimates

• 59 countries still use death penalty, 138 don't

• At least 8,864 sentenced to death in 52 countries

• At least 2,390 people executed in 25 countries

© **2009 MCT**

Source: Amnesty International   Graphics: Jutta Scheibe, Eeli Polli

http://filipspagnoli.files.wordpress.com/2009/06/death-penalty-map.jpg

QUESTION 3 (B) (CONTINUED)

SOURCE 3

A British man Akmal Shaikh, convicted of drug smuggling in China, was executed in December 2009. He had denied any wrongdoing. The execution took place despite protests from his family and the British government. His family argued that he suffered from a mental health condition called bipolar disorder and that this had allowed him to be tricked into carrying the drugs into China.

UK Prime Minister said he condemned the execution of Akmal Shaikh in the strongest terms, and that he was particularly concerned that no mental health assessment was undertaken. The UK continues to oppose to the use of the death penalty by any country.

The Chinese embassy in London made a statement saying that Akmal Shaikh was convicted for serious drug trafficking. The amount of heroin he brought into China was 4,030 grams, enough to cause 26,800 deaths. In Chinese law, 50 grams of heroin or above is classed as not for personal use and is punishable by the death penalty.

A report from the official Chinese news agency Xinhua said that China's Supreme People's Court, which is responsible for monitoring the use of executions, had not been provided with any documentation proving that Mr Shaikh had a mental health disorder.

Based on http://news.bbc.co.uk/1/hi/uk/8433285.stm and http://news.bbc.co.uk/1/hi/world/asia-pacific/8433300.stm

The use of the death penalty is supported by most Chinese people, especially for crimes like murder. China only executes violent criminals. Other countries like Iran use the death penalty more than China. China's Supreme People's Court now monitors the use of executions but they can't overturn a death sentence once it has been passed.

View of Mei Ling

Read the 'View of Mei Ling'.

Fully explain the extent to which Mei Ling could be accused of being selective in the use of facts.

In your answer, you can only use the information in the sources above.

8 marks, Enquiry Skills

SYLLABUS AREA 4—INTERNATIONAL RELATIONS

QUESTION 4

(a)

> A number of groups and political parties within EU member states campaign for their country to leave EU membership.

Fully explain why some groups campaign for their home country to leave the EU.

4 marks, Knowledge and Understanding

(b)

> The UK Government tries to meet the needs of people in some African countries.

Fully describe the methods by which the UK Government helps to meet the **needs** of people in some African countries.

4 marks, Knowledge and Understanding

(c) Examine the four sources then answer the question below.

SOURCE 1

Background

NATO in Afghanistan

NATO's main role in Afghanistan is to assist the Afghan Government and pave the way for reconstruction. NATO commands the UN approved International Security Assistance Force (ISAF). Since NATO took over command in 2003, the number of troops has grown from 5,000 to 70,000. There are troops from 43 countries, including all 28 NATO members.

As well as deploying troops many NATO countries have provided training, funding and equipment for the Afghan National Army. Equipment donations have included 2,000 body armour kits and helmets from Luxembourg. Canada has sent 2,500 guns and 6 million rounds of ammunition. Other countries have sent uniforms, tanks and helicopters.

Selected Security Goals of NATO / ISAF:

1. Promoting security, stability and safety

2. Supporting the Afghan National Army (ANA) in promoting security

3. Disarming illegally armed groups including al Qaeda and Taliban fighters

(Adapted from – http://www.nato.int/cps/en/natolive/topics_8189.htm and http://www.nato.int/isaf/topics/factsheets/ana-equipment-support-factsheet.pdf)

QUESTION 4 (CONTINUED)

SOURCE 2

NATO/ISAF Troop Deployment 2009

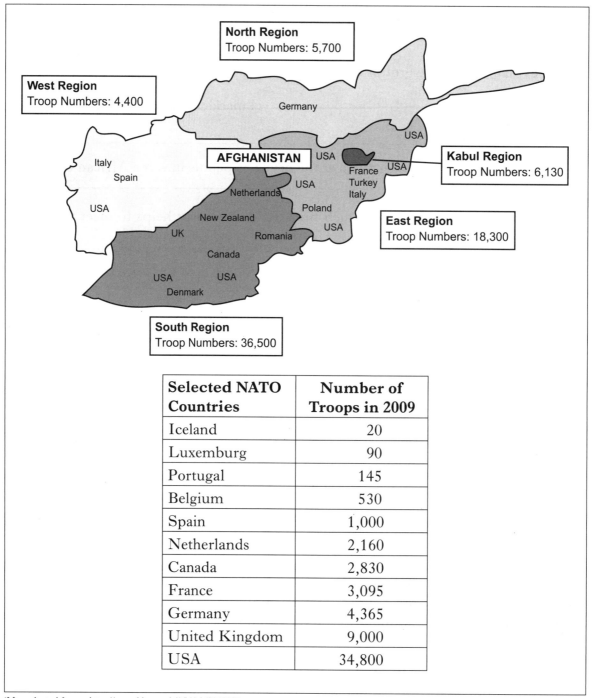

Selected NATO Countries	Number of Troops in 2009
Iceland	20
Luxemburg	90
Portugal	145
Belgium	530
Spain	1,000
Netherlands	2,160
Canada	2,830
France	3,095
Germany	4,365
United Kingdom	9,000
USA	34,800

(Map adapted from – http://news.bbc.co.uk/1/hi/uk/8143196.stm
table information selected from – http://www.nato.int/isaf/docu/epub/pdf/placemat.pdf)

QUESTION 4 (CONTINUED)

SOURCE 3

NATO/ISAF Fatalities in Afghanistan

Year	US	UK	Other	Total
2001	12	0	0	12
2002	49	3	17	69
2003	48	0	9	57
2004	52	1	7	60
2005	99	1	31	131
2006	98	39	54	191
2007	117	42	73	232
2008	155	51	89	295
2009	318	107	94	519
Total	948	244	374	1566

NATO/ISAF Fatalities in Afghanistan in 2009 by Province

Province	NATO/ISAF Fatalities in 2009
Kabul	21
West Region	21
North Region	12
South Region	268
East Region	109

(This table excludes those who died of injuries after being transported back to their home country)

Afghan Civilian Deaths

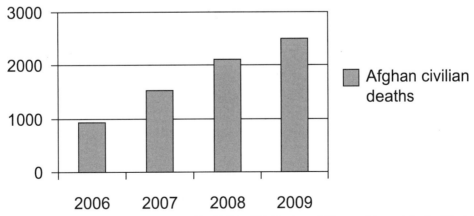

(From – http://www.guardian.co.uk/news/datablog/2009/nov/19/afghanistan-civilian-casualties-statistics-data#data)

QUESTION 4 (CONTINUED)

SOURCE 4

Support for the Afghan National Army (ANA)

NATO Trust Fund Selected Countries	Contributions 2007–2009 in Euros
Belgium	0
Canada	0
France	0
Iceland	0
Portugal	0
Luxembourg	5,726,000
USA	99,964
Spain	4,000,000
United Kingdom	4,540,006
Netherlands	10,600,000
Germany	(Not yet paid in full) 50,000,000

(Information selected from www.nato.int/isaf/topics/ana/index.html)

Make and justify conclusions about the conflict in Afghanistan using the four headings below.

- Progress towards promoting safety in Afghanistan
- Support for the Afghan Army
- The commitment of NATO members to Afghanistan
- The level of danger in different parts of Afghanistan

In your answer, you can only use the information in the sources above.

8 marks, Enquiry Skills

[End of Question Paper]

General Level Exam B

Modern Studies

Standard Grade: General Level

Practice Papers
For SQA Exams

General Level
Exam B

1. You have 1 hour 30 minutes to complete the exam.

2. Try to answer all of the questions in the time allowed.

3. For Question 3 you should only answer ONE section:

Either Section A – The USA
Or Section B – China

SYLLABUS AREA 1—LIVING IN A DEMOCRACY

QUESTION 1

MPs represent their constituents in many ways.

(a) Fully describe **two** ways in which MPs **represent** their constituents in the House of Commons.

4 marks, Knowledge and Understanding

(b) Examine the sources then answer the question below.

SOURCE 1
The number of Trade Union members in selected Trade Unions by gender (2010)

Trade Union	Male Members	Female Members	Total Members
CWU	189,679	47,546	237,225
GMB	326,037	264,088	590,125
RMT	66,862	9,044	75,906
UNISON	403,200	940,800	1,344,000
UNITE	1,506,057	446,453	1,952,510

SOURCE 2
Trade Union Participation Survey Result

Question: Which of the following reasons would make you join a Trade Union?

Reason	Male	Female
Negotiate better pay	37%	21%
Negotiate better working conditions such as more holidays or improved health and safety	23%	46%
Provide training for new skills	30%	13%
Promote lifelong learning, provide legal and financial advice	8%	5%
Provide help and advice with problems at work	12%	15%

Men make up the majority of Trade Union Membership. The main reason why women join a Trade Union is to negotiate better pay.

View of Kevin McNeill

Read the 'View of Kevin McNeill'.

Give **one** reason to support and **one** reason to oppose this view.

In your answer, you can only use the information in the sources above.

4 marks, Enquiry Skills

QUESTION 1 (CONTINUED)

(c)

> Members of pressure groups have many rights when campaigning.

Describe **two rights** that a member of a pressure group has when campaigning.

Select **one** of these rights and explain the **responsibility** that goes with it.

4 marks, Knowledge & Understanding

(d) Examine the source and then answer the question below.

Background of MPs by Political Party (NUMBER)

	1997			2005		
	Cons	**Lab**	**Liberal Democrat**	**Cons**	**Lab**	**Liberal Democrat**
Women	13	101	3	17	98	10
Ethnic Minorities	0	9	0	2	13	0
Professional Occupation	126	225	34	76	141	25
Manual Profession	1	54	1	1	35	0
Total Number of MPs	165	419	46	198	356	62

Write **one** conclusion for each of the following:

- The political party with the biggest change in occupation of their MPs from 1997 to 2005

- The change in women and ethnic minority MPs from 1997 to 2005

Give evidence for each of your conclusions.

In your answer, you can only use the information in the source above.

4 marks, Enquiry Skills

SYLLABUS AREA 2—CHANGING SOCIETY

QUESTION 2

Residential homes help to meet the housing needs of the elderly.

(a) Describe **two** ways in which residential homes can help meet the **needs** of the elderly.

4 marks, Knowledge and Understanding

(b) Examine the sources and then answer the question below.

SOURCE 1

New Deal Leads to More Work Opportunities

The New Deal offers a range of services and benefits designed to get people into work. It is estimated that 62% of young people have been helped into work through the New Deal. Other groups such as single parents (56%), ethnic minorities (22%), older workers (38%) and 61% of disabled workers have also found work as a direct result of the New Deal.

SOURCE 2

Survey of Career Paths of 1,000 People Helped by the New Deal

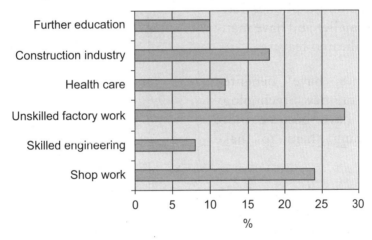

Statements Made by Richard Duncan

- No disabled workers have been helped into work through the New Deal.
- Few people go into further education following the New Deal.
- The New Deal has helped people into work.
- Most people found shop work following the New Deal.

QUESTION 2 (CONTINUED)

Write down **two** statements made by Richard Duncan which are exaggerated.

Then give **one** reason why each of the statements you have chosen is exaggerated.

In your answer, you can only use the information in the sources above.

4 marks, Enquiry Skills

(c) | Some elderly people have fewer illnesses than other elderly people.

Give **two** reasons to explain why some elderly people suffer fewer illnesses than others.

4 marks, Knowledge and Understanding

(d) Examine the two sources then answer the question below.

SOURCE 1

View of Gayle Stewart

New technology has developed rapidly over the past few years. For example, mobile phones have become even smaller and have many new and complicated features.

UK companies have benefited hugely due to new technology because they have become more efficient, helping them to make larger profits.

More profits mean that more jobs will be created which will bring down unemployment rates.

Continued development of technology can only lead to more successful companies.

SOURCE 2

View of Peter Murphy

The development of new technology has made UK companies more efficient.

However, the rate at which new technology is developing will lead to some companies failing because they cannot remain competitive.

If companies cannot remain competitive, they will lose profits and this will lead to a loss of jobs and rising unemployment.

Companies will have to invest heavily in new technology if they want to remain in business.

The sources give different views about new technology.

Write down **two** differences between these views.

In your answer, you can only use the information in the sources above.

4 marks, Enquiry Skills

SYLLABUS AREA 3—IDEOLOGIES

Answer **one** section only: Section (A) USA (Pages 51 to 52)

OR   Section (B) China (Pages 53 to 55)

QUESTION 3
(A) USA

(a) | More ethnic minorities have begun to start up their own businesses. |

Give **two** reasons why more ethnic minorities have begun to start up their own businesses.

You must use American examples in your answer.

4 marks, Knowledge and Understanding

(b) Examine the two sources then answer the question below

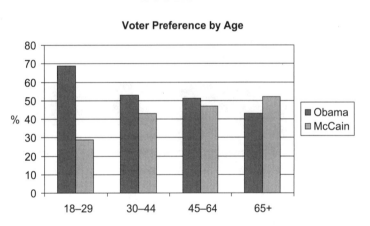

SOURCE 1

Popular Vote 2008 USA
Presidential Election

46%   54%

■ Obama
■ McCain

SOURCE 2

Voter Preference by Age

■ Obama
■ McCain

Adapted from http://www.usatoday.com/news/politics/default.htm

In the 2008 Presidential election, the winner had a clear majority. The winner also received more votes than his opponent in all age ranges.

View of Keir Martin

Read the 'View of Keir Martin'.

Give **one** reason to support and **one** reason to oppose this view.

In your answer, you can only use the information in the sources above.

4 marks, Enquiry Skills

QUESTION 3 (A) (CONTINUED)

 You are investigating the following topic:

> Campaigning in USA Elections.

(*c*) Give **two** appropriate aims for your investigation, as part of the planning stage.

2 marks, Enquiry Skills

A relative gives you the address of a friend who campaigns for a Governor in the USA. You decide to write a letter to her asking what she does to help campaign for the Governor.

(*d*) Give **one** advantage and **one** disadvantage of sending a letter to help with your investigation.

2 marks, Enquiry Skills

Whilst researching your investigation you discover the following website:

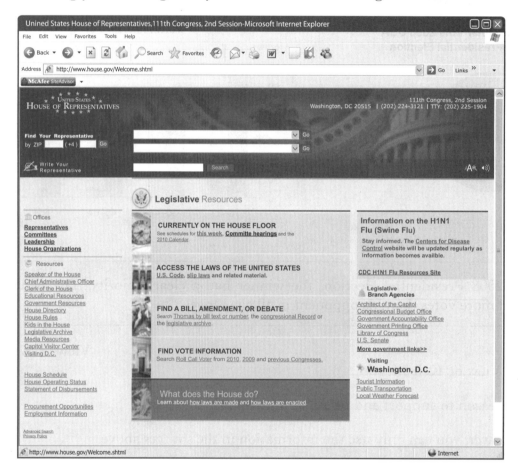

(*e*) Give **two** ways you could use this website to find more information for your investigation. For each way you've chosen, explain why it would be a good way to find out this information.

4 marks, Enquiry Skills

QUESTION 3 (CONTINUED)

QUESTION 3

(B) CHINA

(a) | Chinese people can take part in political activity.

Describe **two** ways that Chinese people can take part in political activity.

4 marks, Knowledge and Understanding

(b) Examine the two sources then answer the question below.

SOURCE 1

CO_2 Pollution Levels in China and the USA in Millions of Tons

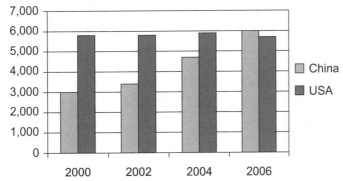

QUESTION 3 (B) (CONTINUED)

SOURCE 2

Cumulative CO$_2$ Emissions, 1960–2005 % of World Total

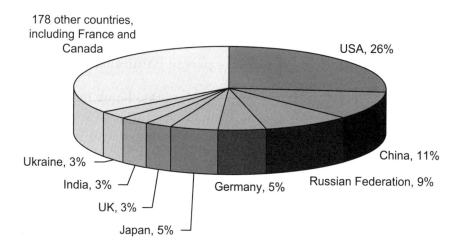

Based on http://climateprogress.org/2009/06/01/us-responsible-for-29-of-carbon-dioxide-emissions-over-past-150-years-triple-chinas-share/

China has recently overtaken the USA in CO$_2$ pollution. Between 1960 and 2005 China is the fourth worst country for overall CO$_2$ emissions in the world.

View of Rachel Bennie

Read the 'View of Rachel Bennie'.

Give **one** reason to support and **one** reason to oppose this view.

In your answer, you can only use the information in the sources above.

4 marks, Enquiry Skills

QUESTION 3 (B) (CONTINUED)

You are investigating the following topic:

Freedom of Information in China

(c) Give **two** appropriate aims for your investigation as part of the planning stage.

2 marks, Enquiry Skills

Human Rights groups like Amnesty International monitor and report on rights and freedoms in different countries. You decide to find out if Amnesty International has information which you could use to help you with your investigation.

(d) Give **two** methods that you could use to find out information from Amnesty International.

For each method you have chosen, explain why it is a good method to get information to help you with your investigation.

4 marks, Enquiry Skills

Your teacher shows you a recording of a BBC Panorama television programme called 'China's Olympic Promise'. The programme investigated the promise of the Chinese Government that the foreign media would be free to report on Chinese politics, economics and society in the build-up to the Olympic Games. The programme was broadcast in August 2008.

(e) Give **one** advantage and **one** disadvantage of using this television programme for your investigation.

2 marks, Enquiry Skills

QUESTION 3 (B) (CONTINUED)

SYLLABUS AREA 4—INTERNATIONAL RELATIONS

QUESTION 4

(*a*)

> Membership of NATO continues to be a benefit

Describe, in detail, the ways in which NATO membership continues to meet the **needs** of member countries.

4 marks, Knowledge and Understanding

(*b*) Examine the two sources then answer the question below.

SOURCE 1—DFID in Malawi

Malawi is home to over 13 million people, 40% of whom live below the poverty line. In 2009/2010, DFID (UK Government Department of International Development) will provide aid to Malawi totalling £75 million. DFID support has helped the country reduce the deaths of under-5s by more than 10% since 2004. In Malawi DFID's support has led to 4200 classrooms being built, 18 million textbooks given to schools and built 315 teacher training centres.

Adapted from http://www.dfid.gov.uk/where-we-work/africa-eastern--southern/malawi/

SOURCE 2—DIFD spending in selected African Countries

Country	DFID Spending in £millions (2007/08)
Sudan	62·7
DR Congo	39·4
Uganda	18·4
Malawi	1·9
Mozambique	1·8
Zambia	1·6

Based on http://www.dfid.gov.uk/Documents/publications/africa-humanitarian-spend-analysis-2007-08.pdf

QUESTION 4 (CONTINUED)

Statements made by James Douglas

Very few people live in poverty in Malawi.

DFID has helped improve education in Malawi by building classrooms and training teachers.

DFID spent more money on Malawi in 2007/08 than on any other African County.

In 2007/08 DFID spent almost £2 million on Malawi.

Read the statements made by James Douglas.

Write down **two** statements which are exaggerated.

Then give **one** reason why each of the statements you have chosen is exaggerated.

In your answer, you can only use the information in the sources above.

4 marks, Enquiry Skills

(c)

| Tied Aid |
| Voting in the UN |

Give **two** reasons why developed countries give aid to some African countries.

You may wish to use the headings above in your answer.

4 marks, Knowledge and Understanding

(d) Examine the information then answer the question below.

Background:

The European Union (EU) gives money to help a number of projects across Scotland including the Highlands and Islands.

The EU uses key priorities to help it decide what projects to fund.

In the Highlands and Islands priorities include:

- Ensuring that everyone has good access to education (e.g. college/university) even if they live somewhere very remote.

- Protecting and promoting the Gaelic language.

- Protecting the local environment (e.g. recycling, reducing car pollution).

- Helping people to find work in their local area and stop them having to move away to find work in towns and cities.

QUESTION 4 (CONTINUED)

- Helping people to find suitable employment, education or training.
- Ensuring equal opportunities for groups and individuals (no discrimination).

The EU needs to decide which project to fund. **Project A** or **Project B**.

PROJECT A

Silean Sgrìobhaidh Gàidhlig – Gaelic Writing Skills

Having already run a successful 'English for Journalists' course, the National Union for Journalists would like an EU grant to develop a course to improve the Gaelic writing skills of journalists and writers in the Highlands and Islands. It is hoped to develop an online course, enabling them to meet the needs of learners across even the most remote parts of the area.

PROJECT B

Hospitality Training for Speakers of English and Polish

This project hopes to improve the skills of people working in the hospitality sector (e.g. in restaurants and hotels). Tourism is very important for the Highlands and Islands and better training could lead to more money and more jobs in tourism.

If more tourists come to the area then more people will be able to find work locally.

In recognition of the large number of Polish speakers employed in the hospitality industry in the region, the project will also provide training materials in Polish.

(all information in this question is based on – http://www.scotland.gov.uk/News/Releases/2006/12/28110451 & http://www.hipp.org.uk/horizthemes.asp.
Minority languages priority from – http://ec.europa.eu/education/languages/languages-of-europe/doc139_en.htm)

Read through the information above and decide which Project (**A** or **B**) would be the better choice for the EU to meet its key priorities.

Give **two** reasons that support your choice of Project.

In your answer you must link the background information to the project you selected.

4 marks, Enquiry Skills

[End of Question Paper]

Credit Level Exam B

Modern Studies

Standard Grade: Credit Level

Practice Papers
For SQA Exams

Credit Level
Exam B

1. You have 2 hours to complete the exam.

2. Try to answer all of the questions in the time allowed.

3. For Question 3 you should only answer **one** section:

Either Section A – The USA
Or Section B – China

SYLLABUS AREA 1—LIVING IN A DEMOCRACY

QUESTION 1

(*a*)

> After joining, a member of a trade union gains many new rights and responsibilities.

Fully explain the **rights and responsibilities** that trade unions have when representing their members.

6 marks, Knowledge and Understanding

(*b*)

> Pressure groups use many methods to influence elected representatives.

Fully explain the ways that pressure groups can influence elected **representatives**.

4 marks, Knowledge and Understanding

(*c*) Examine the three sources then answer the question below.

SOURCE 1

**Extract From the Daily Briton Front Page
'Violence Overshadows Protests at G8 Summit'**

Thousands of protestors took to the streets yesterday to protest at the G8 Summit held in London. The meeting, of the 8 richest countries in the world, was discussing how to deal with debt in the developing world as well as looking to solve the economic crisis that has affected developed countries like the UK. About 250,000 pressure group campaigners took to the streets with banners stating "Justice for the poor", and "No bail out for greedy bankers". A spokesperson for the 'Justice for all' group told our reporter "this is the time to take direct action against governments who are not doing nearly enough to help poorer people". Not all of the protests were peaceful. A small minority of campaigners smashed windows of several high street banks, Estate Agents, coffee shops and other shops and businesses as the demonstration marched to the main city square. At one point, the police and protestors clashed, leading them to close off an area with about 250 protestors in it as they threw missiles at police. There were some arrests, mainly of young men, and some protestors and police officers required hospital treatment for minor facial injuries. A spokesperson for the police service told us that: "there have been some arrests as a result of vandalism of property and attempted assault of some police officers. These people will be charged. However, most of the protestors were clearly law abiding and good natured". Not everybody was happy with the way the protests went however. The Managing Directors of two of the banks who had their premises targeted believe the damage done could end up running into hundreds of thousands of pounds. Disruption to roads and transport was minimal.

QUESTION 1 (CONTINUED)

SOURCE 2

Survey (10,000 people) of Pressure Group Campaign Methods

Question: Have you ever been involved in any of these methods of campaigning?

Method	Male(%)	Female(%)
Signing a petition	6	5
Going on a demonstration	3	4
Writing a letter to a newspaper	15	58
Lobbying MPs, MSPs, or councillors	60	42
Taking direct action	5	1
Boycotting goods or companies	45	56

Percentage of Men Involved in Direct Action (Disruptive Methods)

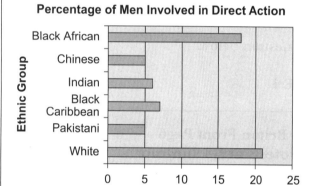

Percentage of Men Involved in Direct Action

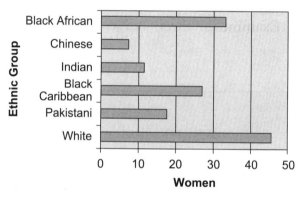

Percentage of Women Involved in Direct Action

SOURCE 3

Economic Impact of Damage Caused by Pressure Groups (£ Millions)		
Type of Damage	All Pressure Groups	'Justice for all' Pressure Group
Lost business	3·7	2·1
Damage to cars	1·3	0·75
Buses	0·3	0·05
Property	0·8	0·4
People (injuries needing hospital treatment)	1·7	0·9

QUESTION 1 (CONTINUED)

SOURCE 3 (CONTINUED)

The Department of Transportation had an annual budget of £18 billion in 2008–09. The department has several aims and is concerned with: 1) delivering reliable and efficient transport networks, 2) looking at transport alternatives that will stop climate change, 3) improving safety and security on roads, rails and air by reducing the risk of death, injury or illness.

Sometimes, when roads are blocked the department of transportation will work together with local police services to get them open again. It is essential to keep Britain's roads open for many reasons, e.g. so that food can get to rural areas and to supermarkets across the country. Where people are involved in irresponsible actions, such as blocking roads to protest, they are not only breaking the law but having a negative impact on people across the United Kingdom.

The most disruptive public event of the year, which forced the road closures of many roads across the capital was the 'FREE GAZA' pressure group when more than half a million people marched in protest over Israel's blockade of GAZA. Other pressure groups such as 'Justice for all' forced road closures mainly around the Westminster area.

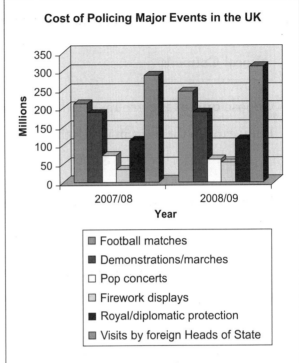

Cost of Policing Major Events in the UK

Legend:
- Football matches
- Demonstrations/marches
- Pop concerts
- Firework displays
- Royal/diplomatic protection
- Visits by foreign Heads of State

Cost of policing the protests at the G8 Summit in 2008/09 = £2.7 million

Policing costs involve:

- Purchase of Specialist equipment
- Overtime payments
- Salaries of police officers
- Transport costs
- Air unit support costs
- Road signs for public safety/road closures

Young white men are the most likely group to be involved in disruptive methods when participating in pressure group activity. 'Justice for all' caused major disruption to the roads and transport network at the G8 Summit. Damage to the UK economy is the biggest impact of pressure group activity.

View of Kate Wilson

Read the 'View of Kate Wilson'.

Fully explain the extent to which this view could be accused of being selective in the use of facts.

In your answer, you can only use the information in the sources above.

8 marks, Enquiry Skills

SYLLABUS AREA 2—CHANGING SOCIETY

QUESTION 2

(a)   **Meeting the Needs of the Elderly**

| Local Councils | | National Government |

Choose **one** of the groups from the options above.

Fully explain the ways in which the group you have chosen meets the **needs** of the elderly.

6 marks, Knowledge and Understanding

(b) Examine the two sources then answer the question below.

SOURCE 1

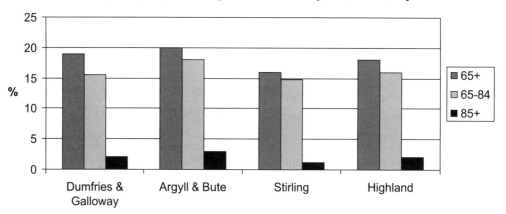

% Elderly Population Aged 65 and Over by Local Authority

SOURCE 2

Estimated Local Authority Cost of Care Services for the Elderly (£000s)		
	2007	**2009**
Dumfries & Galloway	28,500	29,300
Argyll & Bute	19,700	20,100
Stirling	14,900	15,500
Highland	39,800	40,100

The local authority with the biggest % difference between elderly people aged 65+ and 65–84 also had the biggest increase in the cost of care for elderly services. The local authority with the smallest increase in the cost of care was Argyll & Bute.

View of Andrew Goldie

Read the 'View of Andrew Goldie' then give **one** reason to support and **one** reason to oppose this view.

In your answer, you can only use the information in the sources above.

4 marks, Enquiry Skills

QUESTION 2 (CONTINUED)

(c) Examine the information about Glasgow and the four sources then answer the question below.

INFORMATION ABOUT GLASGOW

Focus on Glasgow Electoral Wards

- Glasgow has a population of around 580 000.

- The city is divided into 79 electoral wards.

- More than three quarters of the most deprived areas of Scotland are in Glasgow.

- Glasgow City Council and Glasgow Housing Association (GHA) are working together to invest in several regeneration projects to improve housing conditions for thousands of Glaswegians.

Population of Glasgow: Employment and Benefits (2008)

	Number	%
Benefits claimants	94,600	24·3
On Incapacity Benefit	52,680	13·6
On Income Support	26,780	6·9
In employment	210,648	57·5

Sources adapted from http://www.glasgow.gov.uk/en/AboutGlasgow/Factsheets/Wards

SOURCE 1

Selected Occupation Groups Within Glasgow Electoral Wards (actual numbers and as % of Ward)

	Managers	Skilled Workers	Unskilled Workers
Calton	537 (4·0%)	809 (6·1%)	1,776 (13·3%)
Govan	1,133 (5·9%)	1,328 (6·9%)	2,311 (12·1%)
Hillhead	3,315 (16·7%)	635 (3·2%)	745 (3·8%)
Partick West	3,211 (15·9%)	989 (4·9%)	1,029 (5·1%)
Linn	978 (5·4%)	1,386 (7·7%)	2,155 (11·9%)
Langside	1,937 (12·3%)	997 (6·4%)	943 (6·0%)

QUESTION 2 (CONTINUED)

SOURCE 2

Employment and Benefits in Selected Glasgow Wards (%)

	Linn	Govan	Hillhead	Langside	Calton	Partick West
Benefits claimants	26·9	27·7	12·1	13·8	37·1	15·4
On Incapacity Benefit	14·5	15·7	6·4	7·7	22·4	9·1
On Income Support	8·0	7·3	3·2	3·5	8·8	3·6
In employment	58·3	55·5	61·4	74·6	44·7	68·7

SOURCE 3

Life Expectancy in Selected Glasgow Electoral Wards (years)

	Calton	Govan	Hillhead	Partick West	Langside	Linn
Male	61·9	67	70·4	72·3	73·6	73·9
Female	74·6	75·4	77·5	79·4	78·7	75·3

SOURCE 4

Housing Statistics in Selected Glasgow Wards (%)

	Owner Occupied	Private Rented	Social Rented
Linn	52·8	6·5	40·8
Govan	41·0	14·4	44·7
Hillhead	64·5	25·4	20·1
Langside	71·3	20·7	8·0
Calton	28·0	15·1	56·8
Partick West	58·4	19·0	22·5

Make and justify conclusions about Glasgow and some of its electoral wards using each of the headings below.

- The relationship between occupation and housing

- The relationship between life expectancy and employment

- The electoral ward whose employment statistics are most like that of Glasgow as a whole

- The electoral ward that would be most desirable to live in

In your answer, you can only use the information in the sources and 'Information about Glasgow' above.

8 marks, Enquiry Skills

SYLLABUS AREA 3—IDEOLOGIES

Answer **one** section only: Section (A) USA (Pages 67 to 69)

                              OR   Section (B) China (Pages 70 to 72)

QUESTION 3

(A) USA

(*a*)

> Economic and social inequalities continue to cause problems for some ethnic groups within the USA.

Fully explain how economic and social inequalities continue to cause problems for some ethnic groups within the USA.

You must use American examples in your answer.

8 marks, Knowledge and Understanding

(*b*) Examine the Health Care Debate Information and the two sources then answer the question below

The Health Care Debate – Information

Paying for health care is a major issue for all countries and some spend a lot more than others to keep their citizens healthy. Some countries, like the USA, rely heavily on private insurance companies to provide health care but the problem with this system is that many people feel they cannot afford private insurance or that they simply do not need it and decide not to take it out. As costs have increased, millions of Americans have found themselves unable to afford health insurance and government spending on providing care for the poor and elderly has risen substantially.

A health care bill with an estimated cost of over £650 billion has been passed in the USA that promises to provide health cover to 31 million of the 36 million Americans who currently do not have any cover at all. For this reason, President Barack Obama made reform of the American health care system his top priority when he entered the White House.

The bill will reduce government spending by an estimated 132 billion dollars over the first 10 years and as much as 1.3 trillion dollars during the following 10 years. Over 70% of bankruptcies in the USA are estimated to be due to medical bills that cannot be paid and the new health plan is therefore important for the prosperity and welfare of the USA in the long run.

Fifty-eight Democratic senators and two independents backed the health care bill, while every Republican senator voted against it. Republican senators complain that the bill will not lower costs and will simply provide financial support for private insurance companies.

Although the American Medical Association, the USA's largest medical organisation supports the plan, many doctors have left the organisation in protest arguing that the bill will lead to inferior patient care as doctor, surgeries around the country find their patient lists increasing hugely and they become forced to ration care.

QUESTION 3 (A) (CONTINUED)

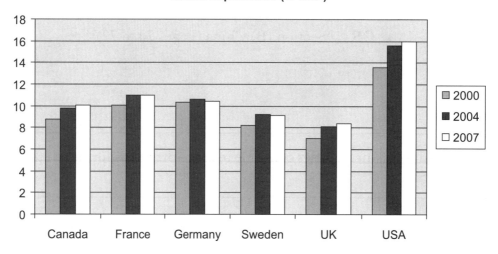

Health Expenditure (% GDP)

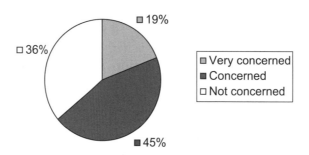

Public Concern on Health care

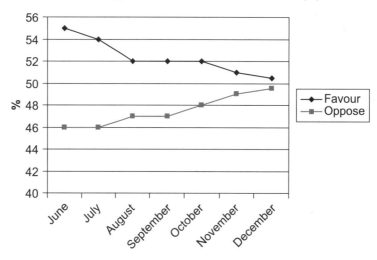

Public Support for Care Plan Jun–Dec 2009 (%)

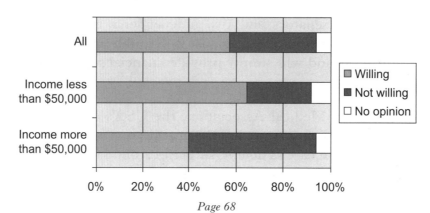

**Public Willingness to Pay
Higher Taxes for New Health Plan**

QUESTION 3 (A) (CONTINUED)

SOURCE 1

View of Graham Green

I have lived and worked in the USA all my life and, like most Americans, I am concerned that a rich country like ours does not provide health cover for so many of our citizens.

Health care is a very important issue and it is clear that the majority of the American public supports President Obama's health care plan.

I will support the health plan because the current government expense as a % of GDP is much greater than that of other countries and needs to be reduced.

Political opposition to the bill is not clear and this demonstrates the general support that exists for the bill.

Nobody likes paying more tax, but everyone is willing to pay higher taxes in order to pay for health cover for our citizens.

SOURCE 2

View of Sarah Heart

I will not support the health plan because it will cost the government money rather than saving it. Even the estimated savings are so low, the benefits do not outweigh the disadvantages.

Americans who earn over $50,000 a year already contribute heavily in taxes to pay for health care for the poor and they clearly do not support the bill.

The use of private insurance companies currently provides a perfectly good system of health care insurance for all American citizens.

Doctors are the experts in this field and their views should be listened to. Many doctors are very unhappy with President Obama's health plan.

Public opposition to the bill has been rising as more details emerge about the costs and disadvantages of the health plan.

State which person's view you agree with most.

Give **three** detailed reasons to support your choice.

Give **two** detailed reasons why you rejected the other person.

In your answer, you must relate the information on the Health Care Debate to the views in the sources above.

10 marks, Enquiry Skills

QUESTION 3 (CONTINUED)

(B) CHINA

(a)

> There are many social and economic inequalities in China.

Fully explain the social and economic inequalities which exist in China.

You must use Chinese examples in your answer.

8 marks, Knowledge and Understanding

(b) Health Care in China

Cost: The Chinese government plans to spend 850 billion Yuan in the next three years (2010–2012) to provide accessible and affordable health care to the people of China.

History: China reformed its health care system in 1992 when it moved from a government run and funded system to a system of health insurance. However, the increased medical costs caused many Chinese people to become poorer. Public complaints have increased because of medical costs, inaccessibility to medical services and low levels of medical insurance coverage. The current system is unpopular and needs to be changed. (Xinhua News Agency January 22, 2009)

Plan: The State Council has approved the final draft of the health care reform at its executive meeting. The aim of the reform is to make the government pay most of the medical expenses of the people by 2011. In the new plan, the government promises to set up a "safe, effective, convenient and affordable" health care system that would cover all urban and rural citizens.

Concerns: Most Doctors have welcomed the reform, but some expressed concern over its long-term effects. "I wonder whether the reform can really spread the insurance cover to rural areas," said Yan Yinlan, a rural doctor in Shanxi Province. Currently about 400 million people do not have any kind of health care cover, according to the Ministry of Health.

Consultation: In 2006, the Government set up a joint working team consisting of experts from 16 government departments to create a reform plan. It also asked organisations, including the World Health Organization, to conduct independent research. The submitted opinions were included in the health care reform plan. In 2007, a government website invited public opinion on the reforms. The website received 1,500 suggestions and 600 letters in less than six months. Key Government leaders have also had meetings with representatives from the medical professions, pharmaceutical companies, and ordinary workers in urban and rural areas. (Xinhua News Agency October 16, 2008)

QUESTION 3 (B) (CONTINUED)

Pharmaceuticals: Health care reforms in China are expected to cause an even more rapid growth in the pharmaceutical (medical drugs) industry in the country. The pharmaceutical market in China expanded 26% in 2008 and is continuing to grow as a result of changes to health care. This will make more money for the economy of China and will therefore be of benefit to everyone. It will also mean that patients have more drug options but some drugs might become more expensive.

Information adapted from http://en.chinagate.cn/top_news/2009-01/22/content_17166908.htm and http://en.chinagate.cn/news/2008-10/16/content_16618264.htm

Growth in Value of Chinese Pharmaceuticals in Billions of US $

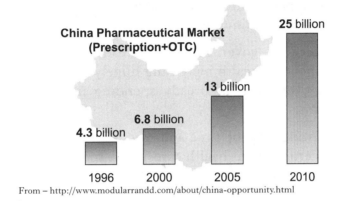

From – http://www.modularrandd.com/about/china-opportunity.html

Government Spending on Health Care in China – Billion Yuan

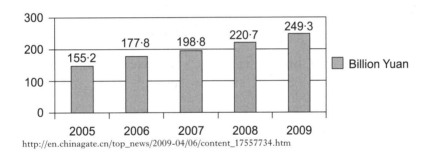

http://en.chinagate.cn/top_news/2009-04/06/content_17557734.htm

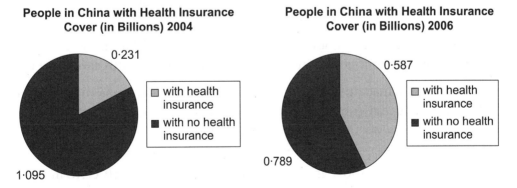

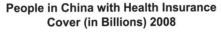

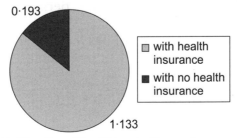

http://www.issa.int/aiss/News-Events/News/Chinese-health-care-reforms-move-towards-universal-coverage

QUESTION 3 (B) (CONTINUED)

SOURCE 1

View of Song Li

The health care reforms require a lot more consideration. I am concerned that they will not help people in rural parts of China.

I think it is the pharmaceutical companies who will make the most money out of any reforms and this will not help ordinary Chinese people.

Most of the 1,326 million people in China are already covered by health care insurance and the numbers covered are continuing to increase.

Health is an area in which the government has already made real improvements with the amount of money spent on health increasing hugely in recent years. We don't need further change. The Government is already spending more on health care without introducing these reforms.

The Government is wasting a lot of time and resources on this issue when clearly the public are not very concerned about health care.

SOURCE 2

View of Lin Yayang

The health care reforms in China have been very well thought through with many different groups involved in the consultation process.

Like many people in China I am very concerned about health care and want to see improvements.

Currently many millions of Chinese do not have any health care cover this is not acceptable. The Government must act to sort this worrying problem.

The Government is not spending enough money on health care. They spent less in 2009 than they did in 2005. The government has not made any changes to health care since the 1950s.

I don't mind if the pharmaceutical companies make more money as this will benefit the country as a whole as these companies will have to pay more tax. People in China will also get better access to a wider range of medical drugs.

State which person's view you most agree with on the issue of Health Care in China.

Give **three** detailed reasons to support your choice.

Give **two** detailed reasons why you rejected the other person.

In your answer you must relate information about Health Care in China to the views in the sources above.

10 marks, Enquiry Skills

SYLLABUS AREA 4—INTERNATIONAL RELATIONS

QUESTION 4

(a)

> The UN aims to promote peace.

Fully describe the ways in which the United Nations can promote peace.

8 marks, Knowledge and Understanding

 You are investigating the following topic:

> **Terrorism and the UK**

(b) State an appropriate hypothesis.

2 marks, Enquiry Skills

(c) Give **two aims/headings that will** help you prove or disprove your hypothesis.

2 marks, Enquiry Skills

(d) Fully describe **two** factors that must be considered when designing and carrying out a survey.

4 marks, Enquiry Skills

QUESTION 4 (CONTINUED)

(*e*) You use the internet to collect more information for your investigation.

You find the Home Office website shown below.

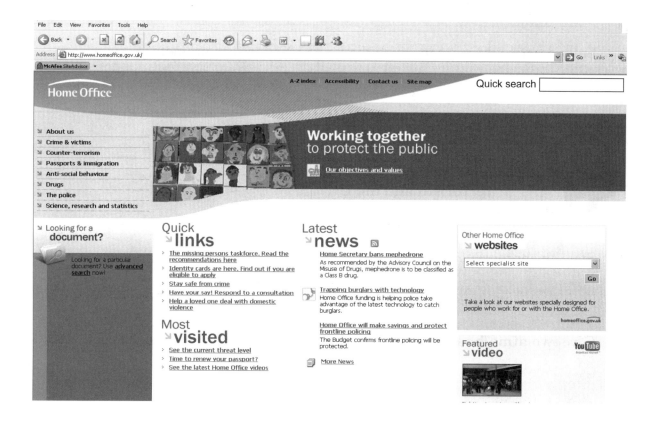

Explain how you would use this website to help in your investigation.

2 marks, Enquiry Skills

[End of Question Paper]

Worked Answers

SYLLABUS AREA 1 – LIVING IN A DEMOCRACY

> **HINT** Remember to refer to the introduction section for more information on answering the questions.

QUESTION 1

> **TOP EXAM TIP**
>
> Nationally, pupils in Modern Studies usually do less well in their Knowledge and Understanding answers than in the Enquiry Skills section. You must make sure you revise all sections thoroughly.

1. (*a*)

> The concept being assessed here is **Rights and Responsibilities**. You are required to give detailed descriptions to achieve full marks. Your answer should start by linking to the question.

A trade union member can support their union during a dispute to increase pay by taking part in a ballot to decide action. This would mean that they would have the responsibility to accept the majority decision in the ballots. e.g. if 2/3 wanted to take action (such as strike action) then everyone would have to do this.

Another way that a trade union member can support their union is to peacefully picket outside their place of work. However they have the responsibility not to intimidate any worker who tries to enter the place of work who is not part of the strike, they should act within the law.

4 marks, Knowledge and Understanding

> **HINT** In this section of the exam you should prepare for questions about the key concepts of **Representation, Participation** and **Rights and Responsibilities**.

> **TOP EXAM TIP**
>
> Watch the time – you only have about 20 minutes in the General exam for each question area.

(*b*)

> In this type of question you need to make comparisons within sources and draw valid conclusions. You can be awarded up to two marks for each difference depending on the quality of your explanation. Two differences are needed for full marks.
>
> You must quote from both sources to show a difference.

Correct responses could include:

Difference 1:
Source 1 says "Voter turnout was the lowest it had ever been for a Scottish Parliament election with only 52% of people voting."

Source 2 says "Voter turnout was low but not as low as it had been in 2003 when it was 49%."

Difference 2:
Source 1 says "There was no difference in the voter turnout in each of the 8 Parliamentary regions. At least more than half of the electorate turned out to vote in all the regions."

Source 2 says "Voter turnout varied quite significantly across the Parliamentary regions. For example, in the West of Scotland region 56.8% turned out to vote whereas in Glasgow region only 43.2% of people voted."

4 marks, Enquiry Skills

> **HINT** Remember you must quote from both sources to show a difference.

1. (continued)

(c)

In this question, you need to give relevant aims for an investigative topic.

Depending on the quality and relevance of your answer, one mark will be awarded for each aim.

You need to give two aims in order to get full marks.

The following aims would receive 0 marks:

- To find out about women in the Scottish Parliament

- To find out about the Scottish Parliament.

The following aims would receive 1 mark:

- To find out the percentage of women MSPs there are for each political party

- To find out if women are more likely to become cabinet ministers than men

- To find out the number of Members' Bills that have been introduced by women MSPs

- Any other valid aim.

2 marks, Enquiry Skills

 HINT > Check that your aims relate to the topic you have been given and try and include reference to a concept, e.g. representation.

(d)

In this question, you need to *state* and then *justify* an appropriate method of enquiry. One mark will be given for each correct method and one mark will be given for each correct advantage. You need to address two methods in order to get full marks.

Correct responses could include:

- Write a letter and send it to the constituency office or Parliament as this would allow you to ask detailed questions and the MSP would have time to respond.

- Send an email as you could have lots of detailed questions and the MSP can email you back because they will have your email address.

- Telephone them as this is a quick way of getting information, you wouldn't need to wait for a response.

- Visit the local constituency office as this would allow face-to-face contact, making it more personal and you could ask lots of open and closed questions and record the information at the same time.

- Visit the surgery as this would allow face-to-face contact, making it more personal and you could ask lots of open and closed questions and record the information at the same time.

- Any other valid point.

4 marks, Enquiry Skills

(e)

In this question, you need to *state* and then *justify* an appropriate method of enquiry. You will be awarded up to two marks for stating a way in which the Internet could be used to help with your investigation. Make sure your answer is relevant to the question, is accurate and has enough detail to get the marks.

Correct responses could include:

- you could search by typing in key words to a search engine such as www.google.co.uk and type in key words like "women", "MSPs", "Parliament"

- once you have found relevant information you could copy and paste it into a new word document, then print it off to refer to later.

- any other valid point.

2 marks, Enquiry Skills

 HINT > In this type of question you may be asked to state advantages or disadvantages for a range of methods. You will need to know the benefits and limitations of all common research methods. You will also need to understand how to use each method effectively. Methods include: interviews, internet, surveys / questionnaires, letters, emails, libraries, newspapers, databases and observational visits.

SYLLABUS AREA 2 – CHANGING SOCIETY

QUESTION 2

> **TOP EXAM TIP**
>
> You don't need to do the whole exam paper in order. Look at the whole paper and start with the question area you think you will do best in. You should aim to keep question areas together, e.g. answer all of Area 3, then all of Area 1 and so on.

2. (a)

 The concept being assessed here is **Need**. You need to give detailed descriptions to get the marks. Two ways are required for full marks. Make sure that your answer specifically refers to young people. It is a good idea to start by linking to the question.

One way that the government tries to help young unemployed people find jobs is by providing Modern Apprenticeships. This enables young people to be trained in a particular trade or skill and gives them qualifications. There are many different types of apprenticeship. Examples of Modern Apprenticeships include engineers and electricians.

Another way that the government helps young people find a job is through the Skillseekers programme where young people between 16-18 are offered training for two years. Young people gain qualifications when they are on the programme, which means they are much more employable and more able to get full-time work.

4 marks, Knowledge and Understanding

HINT ▷ In this section of the exam you should prepare for questions about the key concepts of **Ideology**, **Equality** and **Need**.

> **TOP EXAM TIP**
>
> Read all the questions carefully – make sure you understand what you are being asked.

(b)

 The concept being assessed here is **Equality**. You need to give detailed descriptions in your answer to get full marks. It is a good idea to start your answer by linking to the question.

Points that could feature in your answer include:

- Older workers

    ○ Might face prejudice from employers.

    ○ Might be more expensive for employers to retrain, especially if technological skills are poor.

    ○ May need to be paid more so more expensive for an employer to take on.

    ○ Less flexible in terms of being able to move to a different location.

- Single parents

    ○ Less flexible in relation to working hours and holidays.

    ○ May not be able to move to a different location if company thinks it is necessary.

    ○ Need to take into account child-care arrangements, meaning they would be less likely to work overtime.

    ○ Might have been out of work for a long time looking after children so skills might not be up to date.

4 marks, Knowledge and Understanding

> **TOP EXAM TIP**
>
> Do not write your answers as lists or bullet points. Write in proper sentences.

2. (continued)

(c)

> This is an 'Option choice' type of question where you need to make a clear choice.
>
> To get full marks in your answer you need find two pieces of evidence to support your choice and you need to link your evidence about the programme clearly to the background information.
>
> Answers that do not make a clear link between the programme choice and the background information can only get a maximum of two marks out of four. You must remember to link!

Correct responses could include:

I choose Programme A – Community Development

This would be the best choice for these reasons:

✓ Local companies will improve the quality of housing in the poorest areas within the Health Authority. This can be linked to the areas of deprivation within the Health Authority that suffer poor housing, which contributes to poor health.

✓ Providing free leisure facilities in deprived areas will provide more opportunities for the unemployed to take more regular exercise. This links to the increasing numbers of unemployed people who fail to take regular exercise

OR

I choose Programme B – Healthy Lifestyles

This would be the best choice for these reasons:

✓ NHS nurses will be employed in areas of high unemployment to help smokers give up their habit. This links to the increasing numbers of unemployed people who smoke.

✓ A team of fitness experts will offer free evening training sessions at a range of local schools in deprived areas. This links to the increasing numbers of unemployed people who fail to take regular exercise.

4 marks, Enquiry Skills

HINT

> In this type of question don't waste time trying to decide which option is the best. There is no right or wrong option. Either programme could be chosen as there is enough information to support both. It is how you support your choice and how you link it to the background information that gets you the marks.
>
> Remember that the question tells you to give two reasons in support of your choice, so don't forget to give two points. The answers above have been set out with two sentences for each point. The first sentence refers to the programme information. The second sentence links it to the background information. This is the best way to set out your answer.

(d)

> In this type of question you need to disagree with a given point of view, giving valid reasons for doing so. You need to give two pieces of evidence in order to get full marks. Each relevant piece of evidence in your answer will receive two marks. For full marks you must take account of both sentences in the 'View'. You also have to make a clear link between the 'View' and the information in the table.

Disagree with the view
Graham Black says "Free health care has always been seen as the most important service that they needed."

Evidence to prove
Free health care was seen as most important in 2005 and 2007. However in 2009 23·1% of people considered free health care as most important, whilst 24·8% thought that a heating allowance was the most important service that they needed.

Disagree with the view
Graham Black says "Between 2007 and 2009, the service with the biggest rise in importance was meals on wheels"

Evidence to prove
Meals on wheels rose in importance from 8·8% in 2007 to 10·4% in 2009, a rise of 1·6%, however flu vaccinations rose from 6·4% in 2007 to 9·1% in 2009, which is a bigger rise of 2·7%.

4 marks, Enquiry Skills

SYLLABUS AREA 3 – IDEOLOGIES USA OR CHINA

QUESTION 3A – THE USA

> **TOP EXAM TIP**
>
> Do not write your answers as lists or bullet points. Write in proper sentences.

3A. *(a)*

> The concept being assessed in this question is **Participation**. You have to show understanding of the concept. You can get up to three marks for each individual point depending on how well you describe and explain it. Two descriptions are required for full marks. If you do not give an American example, you will only receive a maximum of three marks. Including more relevant details in your answer will improve the marks you are awarded.
>
> Each of the bullet points below makes a point and backs up the point. Two of these bullet points would be enough to get you full marks. It is a good idea to open your answer with a link to the question.

Link: American people can influence the government through interest groups by:

- Allowing American people to join forces and create a more powerful voice to help ensure their views are made known to the government.

- Focusing upon a single issue, such as gun control (e.g. The Coalition to Stop Gun Violence), or a particular social group, such as the elderly (e.g. 60 Plus Association).

- Taking direct action. For example, the coalition group Witness Against Torture demonstrated outside the White House to campaign for the closure of Guantanamo prison.

- Advertising campaigns through the media to gain public support and influence the government. For example, the AARP (American Association of Retired Persons) ran a TV campaign to support health care reform.

4 marks, Knowledge and Understanding

> *HINT* In this section of the exam you should prepare for questions about the key concepts of **Ideology**, **Participation**, **Equality** and **Rights and Responsibilities**.

> **TOP EXAM TIP**
>
> Remember you MUST use American examples in your answers to get a good mark in this section.

(b)

> **Support and oppose type question.**
>
> In this type of question you need to give evidence to support and evidence to oppose the stated point of view. This means that Mary Wardrop says something which is correct and something which is wrong. For four marks you would need to do the following:
>
> To support – you should quote what the person says that is correct.
>
> You should then give evidence from one of the sources to show why it is correct.
>
> To oppose – you should quote what the person says that is wrong.
>
> You should then give evidence from one of the sources to show why it is wrong.
>
> You must clearly link the 'view' to the sources for both your statements, in support and in opposition. If you don't make a clear link between the views and the sources, you will only receive a maximum of two marks.
>
> You must use both sources and you must use both sentences in the 'view' to get full marks.

To support

Mary Wardrop says that "The state of Montana has the lowest unemployment rate of most other selected states".

Evidence to support

Source 2 supports this view as it shows Montana has an unemployment rate of 4.4% which is higher than Colorado, but lower than the other three states.

To oppose

Mary Wardrop says that "the citizens of Montana have both the highest rate of gun ownership and gun deaths". *Note that **both parts** of this statement would have to be true to support Mary Wardrop's view.*

3A. (continued)

Evidence to oppose

Source 1 opposes this view as it shows that although Montana does have the highest rate of gun ownership (52 per 100,000), Arizona had the highest rate of gun deaths (18·1 per 100,000).

4 marks, Enquiry Skills

> **TOP EXAM TIP**
>
> You can be asked this sort of question as support only, oppose only or support and oppose. Make sure you read the question carefully and that you understand what you are being asked to do.

(c)

> The concept being assessed in this question is **Equality**. You have to show understanding of this concept. Two descriptions are required for full marks. If you do not give an American example, you will only receive a maximum of three marks. Including more relevant details in your answer will improve the marks you are awarded.
>
> Each of the bullet points below makes a point and backs up the point. Two of these bullet points would be enough to get you full marks. It is a good idea to open your answer with a link to the question.

Link: Some American people are more affected by crime than others because

- Some ethnic groups have no choice but to live in poor, run down areas (ghettoes) where levels of crime are higher with serious drug problems and gang violence. Black Americans are more likely to be the victims of murder than any other group.

- Wealthy Americans can buy homes in the suburbs where levels of crime are lower and they can afford to spend more on protecting their property. Some even live in protected 'gated communities' where anyone coming into the area is monitored.

- Ethnic minority groups continue to face discrimination and prejudice in their dealings with the police and the justice system. Some ethnic minority groups feel that less effort is made investigating cases where the victim is from an ethnic minority group.

4 marks, Knowledge and Understanding

> **TOP EXAM TIP**
>
> Watch the time – you only have about 20 minutes in the General exam for each question area.

(d)

> In this type of question you have to detect and explain exaggeration.
>
> An exaggeration is a wrong statement.
>
> You will get a mark for each exaggerated statement you correctly identify – you should repeat the exaggeration stating clearly that it is exaggerated.
>
> You will then get another mark for providing evidence to prove it is an exaggerated statement.

Statement 1
"President Obama has done nothing to control how these banks operate."

Reason 1
From Source 1, it says that "President Obama has taken a range of strong measures that will limit the size of large banks."

Statement 2
"our level of debt in the USA is higher than most other rich countries."

Reason 2
From Source 2, it shows that Canada's level of debt is lower, but all other countries in the chart are higher than the USA.

4 marks, Enquiry Skills

3A. (continued)

HINT

The easiest way to do this type of question is to look at each of the statements or views expressed by the person. For each statement or view tick or cross your exam paper to say whether it is correct or wrong based on the table, bar graph or written source you have been given. Check all the statements as this will help you make sure you have the selected the two exaggerated ones.

TOP EXAM TIP

Remember exaggeration means there is something incorrect in the statement.

QUESTION 3B – CHINA

HINT

In this section of the exam you should prepare for questions about the key concepts of **Ideology**, **Participation**, **Equality** and **Rights and Responsibilities**.

TOP EXAM TIP

Do not write your answers as lists or bullet points. Write in proper sentences.

3B. (a)

The concept being assessed here is **Ideology**. You need to give detailed descriptions to get full marks. It is a good idea to start by linking to the question.

Some people in China are better off than others as they are members of the Communist party which means that they are more likely to be successful in business. They are more likely to be allowed to set up a business as the government has adopted a capitalist economic system which allows more people to own businesses and keep any profit they make for themselves.

Some people in China are better off than others as they receive different wages to other workers. Workers who live in large urban areas are more likely to be better paid than workers in rural areas. Cities like Beijing and Shanghai have attracted significant amounts of foreign investment in recent years meaning there is more demand for good workers and more money to pay them.

4 marks, Knowledge and Understanding

TOP EXAM TIP

Remember you MUST use Chinese examples in your answers to get a good mark in this section.

(b)

Support and oppose type question.

In this type of question you need to give evidence to support and evidence to oppose the stated point of view. This means that Yang Jinping says something which is correct and something which is wrong.

To support – you should quote what the person says that is correct. You should then give evidence from one of the sources to show why it is correct.

To oppose – you should quote what the person says that is wrong. You should then give evidence from one of the sources to show why it is wrong.

You must clearly link the 'view' to the sources for both your statements, in support and in opposition.

You must use both sources and you must use both sentences in the view to get full marks.

To support
• Yang Jinping says, "Chinese people do not take global warming as seriously as people in other parts of the world."

Evidence to support
• Source 1 supports this view as it shows that about 40% of Chinese people take global warming seriously. All the other areas shown are higher, with about 90% of people in African countries taking global warming seriously.

To oppose
Yang Jinping says, "The Chinese already get most of their energy from cleaner sources like water, wind and solar power".

Evidence to oppose
Source 2 opposes this part of the view as it says that China currently gets about 70% of its energy from coal, which is not a clean form of energy.

4 marks, Enquiry Skills

3B.   (continued)

> *HINT* — You don't have to worry about the exact figures in a bar graph – it is OK to say 'about 90%' or 'just under' or 'just over 90%'. Make sure you include the unit of measurement. This bar graph shows the information in % so you need to refer to this.

TOP EXAM TIP

You can be asked this sort of question as support only, oppose only or support and oppose. Make sure you read the question carefully and that you understand what you are being asked to do.

(c)

> The concept being assessed here is **Equality**. You need to provide detailed explanations to achieve full marks. Make sure you are focusing on social inequalities and not political inequalities. Social issues include areas like education, health, housing, crime, population movement and immigration. Your answer should start by linking to the question.

Correct answers could include:

A social inequality in China is the difference in education received by Chinese citizens. People who live in rural areas tend to receive a poorer standard of education than people who live in urban areas. Whilst there are many universities in China, people from rural areas are less likely to attend them as they cannot afford the move from the countryside to the cities or afford the fees.

Another social inequality that exists is in health care. Health care is not free in China and access to it can vary depending on whether you live in an urban area or a rural area. There are fewer hospitals and doctors in rural areas meaning that people have to travel long distances just to see a doctor; this can make it less likely that people will visit a doctor until their illness becomes more serious. Some people are rich and can afford the best treatment, including travelling overseas to countries like America to get treated.

TOP EXAM TIP

Watch the time – you only have about 20 minutes in the General exam for each question area.

4 marks, Knowledge and Understanding

(d)

> In this type of question you have to detect and explain exaggeration.
>
> An exaggeration is a wrong statement.
>
> You will get a mark for each exaggerated statement you correctly identify – you should repeat the exaggeration stating clearly that it is exaggerated.
>
> You will then get another mark for providing evidence to prove it is an exaggerated statement.

Exaggerated statement
The first exaggerated statement by Allison Black is when she says "Men aged 36–40 are more likely to go online than any other group."

Evidence
Allison is wrong to say this because in Source 1 it says that 81% of men aged 60 and over go online compared to only about 56% of men 36–40 years old going online.

Exaggerated statement
The second exaggerated statement by Allison Black is when she says "Everyone is very happy about the work of these camps."

Evidence
Allison is wrong to say this because in Source 2 it says that many people are unhappy because some teenagers have been beaten at the camps and one even died.

4 marks, Enquiry Skills

> *HINT* — The easiest way to do this type of question is to look at each of the statements or views expressed by the person. For each statement or view tick or cross on your exam paper to show whether it is correct or wrong based on the table, bar graph or written source or sources you have been given.

TOP EXAM TIP

Remember exaggeration means there is something incorrect in the statement.

SYLLABUS AREA 4 – INTERNATIONAL RELATIONS

HINT ▷ In this section of the exam you should prepare for questions about the key concepts of **Need** and **Power**.

4. (*a*)

> Choose one of the issues only.
>
> In this question the concept is **Need**. You must show that you understand the concept. Notice that the word 'need' is repeatedly used in the sample answer below.
>
> Any one of the sections below would be enough to get full marks. Each section has two distinctly different pieces of information relating to the issue. The sample answer starts by linking clearly to the question.

Link: Improvements in **Promoting peace/Health care/Education** (*as appropriate to your choice*) can help meet the needs of people in many African countries.

Promoting peace: Countries which are affected by civil war or international war will have less money to spend on health care and education. If large amounts of money are being spent on weapons and soldiers then it will be hard for a country to develop and meet the basic needs of its people.

During wartime people often flee their homes and become refugees. This means that they end up living in refugee camps and are not working but are dependent on aid. The Darfur region of Sudan has been badly affected by war and there are over two million refugees. Lasting peace would mean that these people could return home and start farming again and be able to meet their own needs.

Health care: Currently many children in African countries become seriously ill and even die from preventable illnesses like measles and malaria. Better health care would mean that immunisation programmes could prevent some of these illnesses. This would help meet the health needs of people in African countries.

Diarrhoea is a major cause of death for young children in Africa. Providing oral rehydration therapy (ORT) to children with diarrhoea helps replace the salts and fluids they have lost. This would meet the health needs of these sick children.

Education: With better education people are more likely to be able to get a good job and be able to support themselves and their family therefore meeting their own needs in the long term. This not only meets the needs of individuals but it would also help the country as a whole to develop and become richer.

Better education could help to meet the health needs of people as more awareness about health issues such as how to prevent the spread of HIV would mean that fewer people would become infected. This would have a positive impact on the health of a country.

4 marks, Knowledge and Understanding

(*b*)

> **Conclusions type question.**
>
> A conclusion should be a trend or pattern you can see from reading the sources.
>
> In this question you need to clearly state two conclusions based on the bullet points in the question. It is best to have a clear conclusion in one sentence and then a second sentence using evidence from the sources to support your conclusion.

Conclusion
The country in the table with the highest rate of HIV/AIDS is Zimbabwe.

Evidence
In the table, Zimbabwe has a 15·3% HIV/AIDS rate for adults aged 15–49 years which is narrowly higher than Zambia with 15·2% and higher than any other country in the table.

Conclusion
There are higher rates of HIV/AIDS in the towns and cities than in the countryside in all the countries listed.

4.   (continued)

Evidence

The rate is always higher in the towns and cities than in the countryside. For example in Zambia there is a 23·1% rate in the towns and cities compared to a 10·8% rate in the countryside.

HINT — It is a good idea to deal with each conclusion in a separate paragraph.

It is also a good idea to have a highlighter with you in the exam. You can then highlight information in the sources. This can help you pick out comparisons between sources.

TOP EXAM TIP

Remember to make sure you give clear conclusions.

(c)

Pick only one option: NATO or the EU.

The concept being assessed in this question is **Power**. You should show awareness of the concept. Notice that the word 'power' is repeatedly used in the sample answer below.

You can get up to three marks for each individual point, depending on how well you describe and explain it. Usually in a four mark question it is easier to make two points and explain each of them well.

The information below for each organisation would be enough to get full marks. Notice also that the answer starts by linking back to the question.

Link: NATO/The EU (use as appropriate for your choice) play an important military role.

NATO

Collective security: Being in any sort of military alliance means that you have safety in numbers. You have other countries that are going to support and help you if you come under attack. This should make a country feel safer and increase the power of all members. After the 2001 terrorist attacks on the USA, NATO countries responded with offers of help to the USA. The UK would benefit from this if we were directly attacked by an outside group or another country.

Working together: The UK troops in Afghanistan are under the command of NATO. This means that all the countries with troops in Afghanistan, such as the UK, USA and Germany are able to work together. If the UK was in Afghanistan on its own or with only a few other countries it would be in weaker position. This again strengthens the military position and the power of the UK.

EU

Eurofighter: The EU has worked together on the development and manufacture of the Eurofighter. This allowed various EU countries to share the cost of the development. Although countries still need to pay direct costs at the time of ordering the fighters, sharing reduces the overall costs to each country. These new fighters will add to the military defensive power of the UK.

Pirates: In December 2008 the EU launched Operation Atalanta, to protect shipping from piracy in the Gulf of Aden. This is the first time the EU has taken command of a military operation outside of Europe. This operation has helped protect UK ships and UK trade from attack and increases the power of the UK and the other EU countries beyond Europe.

4 marks, Knowledge and Understanding

(d)

In this type of question you have to detect and explain exaggeration.

An exaggeration is a wrong statement.

You will get a mark for each exaggerated statement you correctly identify – you should repeat the exaggeration stating clearly that it is exaggerated.

You will then get another mark for providing evidence to prove it is an exaggerated statement.

4.   **(continued)**

Exaggerated statement

The first exaggerated statement by Grace Wilson is when she says "In the last ten years very few countries have joined the EU."

Evidence

Grace is wrong because in the table it shows that many new members have joined the EU with ten joining in 2004 and two in 2007.

Exaggerated statement

The second exaggerated statement by Grace Wilson is that she says "No other countries are now interested in joining the EU."

Evidence

Grace is wrong because in the table it show that three countries; Croatia, Macedonia and Turkey are hoping to join by 2011.

4 marks, Enquiry Skills

HINT   Check all the statements as this will help you make sure you have the selected the two exaggerated ones.

TOP EXAM TIP

If you have time left you should check through your answers.

SYLLABUS AREA 1 – LIVING IN A DEMOCRACY

QUESTION 1

> **HINT** Remember to refer to the introduction section for more information on answering the questions.

> **HINT** In this section of the exam you should prepare for questions about the key concepts of **Representation**, **Participation** and **Rights and Responsibilities**.

1. *(a)*

 The concept being assessed in this question is **Representation**. You need to use your understanding of the concept to provide explanations in depth and detail. You should write two full points to receive full marks. Your answer should start by linking to the question.

One way that local councillors represent their constituents is by representing their views at the local council through committees. For example, if a constituent had a problem with their council house or wanted more recycling centres to be available in their area, the councillor would be able to highlight these issues with the relevant council officials.

Another way that local councillors might represent their constituents is by drawing the media's attention to a particular issue. For example, attracting the attention of the media might prevent proposed local school closures.

4 marks, Knowledge and Understanding

> **HINT** Nationally, pupils in Modern Studies usually do less well in their Knowledge and Understanding answers. You must make sure you revise all sections thoroughly.

(b)

 The concept being assessed here is **Rights and Responsibilities**. Use your understanding of the concept to give depth and detail to your explanations in your answer. You should write two fully explained points to receive full marks. Your answer should start by linking to the question.

One right that people have in a democracy is the right to vote in elections. They can vote for their local councillors, MSPs, MPs and MEPs. This means that they can have a say in how their country is run. The responsibility that goes with this is to make sure that you use your vote and properly consider the reasons why you could vote for a particular person or political party. Once the results have been announced you should also accept the result even if you disagree with it.

Another right that people have in a democracy is the right to protest when they disagree with a decision their elected representatives have taken. They can do this by joining a pressure group, writing a letter to a newspaper or by contacting their elected representative. However, people in a democracy have the responsibility to make sure that all views are heard and not just their own. You cannot prevent others from giving their opinion even if you disagree with it. You also have the responsibility to act within the law and not harm others just to get your point of view across.

4 marks, Knowledge and Understanding

> **TOP EXAM TIP**
> Watch the time – you have just under 30 minutes in the Credit exam for each question area.

1. **(continued)**

(*c*)

> **Decision making type question.**
>
> In your answer, you need to make a clear choice
>
> To get full marks in this answer you again need to use all the information. Your answers must make explicit links between the background information about Dunbarrie Textile Factory and Sources 1 and 2.
>
> You are asked to choose who you most agree with. There is no right or wrong answer as the evidence supports both views. What matters is how you use the information to support your choice and how you reason your rejection of the other person.
>
> You should clearly link your choice to the background information.

Answers may include:

For Margaret Paterson
- In the survey of members regarding the qualities needed in a shop steward, more than a quarter of the members said that the most important quality is that the person is well liked and has worked in the factory for a long period of time. Margaret is well liked and she has worked in the factory for over 20 years, which is a long time.

- From the information about Dunbarrie textile factory you can see that the main priority of the staff is to protect jobs and that this should be the main priority for the new shop steward. This is especially important as the factory has already seen 284 employees being made redundant. Margaret has said that she has two clear priorities if she were to become shop steward these are to safeguard existing jobs and protect employees from further redundancies. This clearly matches what members are looking for.

- Margaret says that strike action should only be used as a last resort. She has the support of the staff as more than half say it should only be used as a last resort. It is also the case that the management clearly do not respond to threats or strike action as last time workers went on strike it did not end well and did not achieve the aim.

Against Margaret Paterson
- Margaret would like to focus on the working conditions of part-time and female workers. The information about Dunbarrie textile factory shows that there are very few part-time and female workers compared to full-time and male workers. This is clearly not a priority for the factory and would not be the main priority for the majority of workers.

- Margaret believes the main focus should be on improving holiday pay and pension rights but in a recent staff survey more than half the staff (56%) said that job security should be the main priority for the new shop steward.

For Hugh Robinson
- Hugh has experience of being a shop steward in his previous job which means that he will have experience of negotiating with management. He was successful at achieving a new pay agreement in his last job. This is clearly important to Trade Union members with over half saying that previous experience of the job and being a good negotiator are the main qualities they consider when choosing a new shop steward.

- Dunbarrie Textile factory is the main place of employment in the local area and is the only job that can offer real prospects to young people with a significant proportion of the workforce being young. One of Hugh's main concerns is that more training should be targeted at young workers and more money invested in training. This would clearly meet a need of many of the workers at the factory.

- Hugh would also like to see an improvement in the rights of part-time workers in relation to improving pension entitlement and holiday pay. This is clearly an issue with staff at the textile factory as more than a quarter are either part-time or temporary with no pension entitlement or good holiday pay.

Against Hugh Robinson
- Hugh thinks the Union should be looking at strike action immediately and that there is no other action open to the union. He does not have a lot of support for this amongst the membership. In a recent survey, Trade Union members (73%) stated that strikes should only be used as a last resort and that other action should be tried first.

- Hugh wants to focus, not just on improving pay and protecting members from compulsory redundancies, but also on improving the quality of staff training and improving health and safety. In a recent staff survey more than half the staff (56%) said that job security should be the main priority for the new shop steward.

Any other valid point both for and against either candidate.

10 marks, Enquiry Skills

1.   (continued)

> **TOP EXAM TIP**
>
> In this type of question don't waste time trying to decide which option is the best. There is no right or wrong answer. There is always enough evidence to support either choice.

SYLLABUS AREA 2 – CHANGING SOCIETY

> **TOP EXAM TIP**
>
> Do not write your answers as lists or bullet points. Write in proper sentences.

2.   (a)

> The concept being assessed here is **Need**. Again, use your understanding of the concept of 'need' to provide detailed descriptions with relevant examples and appropriate generalisations. You should aim for four clear separate points in this answer to ensure eight marks. Your answer should start by linking to the question.

Answers could include:

One way that the government meets the needs of the unemployed is by providing benefits while they are out of work. This helps to meet their financial needs as they will have little money to pay for essentials whilst they are unemployed. One of the benefits the government provides is Jobseekers' Allowance.

Another way that the government helps meet the needs of the unemployed is by helping them get back into work. This can be done by offering training schemes such as the New Deal, helping with job applications and improving skills through schemes such as Skillseekers.

Another way that the government helps meet the needs of the unemployed is by providing job centres where people can find out about the jobs available, benefits that they might be entitled to and receive help and advice with their applications.

One last way that government can help is by providing a full range of services that meet the social needs of the unemployed such as council housing and the NHS.

8 marks, Knowledge and Understanding

> **HINT**   In this section of the exam you should prepare for questions about the key concepts of **Ideology**, **Equality** and **Need**.

> **TOP EXAM TIP**
>
> Read all the questions carefully – make sure you understand what you are being asked.

(b)

> Questions **2.** (b) to **2.** (e) are an investigation set of questions.
>
> **Hypothesis**
>
> A hypothesis is a statement which can be proved or disproved.
>
> You have to state a hypothesis relevant to the issue of "Elderly people and residential homes."
>
> To get full marks you need to show understanding of the issue.

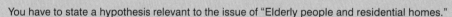

The following would not be acceptable and would get no marks:

*   Do the elderly like residential homes?
*   Elderly people live in residential homes.

The following do not show much understanding and so would receive 1 mark only:

*   Residential homes look after the needs of the elderly.
*   Elderly people feel safer in residential homes.

The following hypotheses would each receive 2 marks:

*   ✓ Residential homes help meet the physical needs of the elderly who are no longer fit enough to live independently.
*   ✓ Residential homes help meet the social needs of the elderly by providing company and preventing loneliness.

These are not the only possible options for this investigation area – see if you can come up with some more hypotheses of your own.

2 marks, Enquiry Skills

2. (continued)

| HINT | Your hypothesis must never be a question. If it has 'what', 'where', 'why', 'who', 'how' or 'when' then it is a question not a hypothesis. |

TOP EXAM TIP

Check carefully that your hypothesis is a statement and not a question.

(c)

Aims

Now you have to come up with aims that are relevant to your hypothesis.

Your aims are what you would need to find out to prove or disprove your investigation hypothesis.

You get one mark for each aim depending on how it relates to the hypothesis.

Hypothesis

"Residential homes help meet the physical needs of the elderly who are no longer fit enough to live independently."

Aims

✓ To find out about the types of physical needs of the elderly.

✓ To find out about the services provided by residential homes.

You may be able to think of some other aims. Try the other hypothesis in the answer to part (b) above and see if you can think of some aims to go with it.

TOP EXAM TIP

Check that your aims are related to your hypothesis.

2 marks, Enquiry Skills

(d)

Interviews

You need to think about advantages and disadvantages of interviewing elderly people in a residential home.

You will get up to two marks for each advantage and disadvantage you make if it is well explained.

Any one advantage and one disadvantage from below would be enough to get full marks.

Advantage

✓ The views of the elderly and their opinions on what it is like to live in a residential home can be explored in detail.

✓ You can immediately follow up interesting points with more detailed questions.

✓ The length of the interview can be flexible depending on how useful the elderly person's responses are to you.

Disadvantage

✓ The elderly person may not understand your questions and give vague answers that do not help your investigation.

✓ Some elderly people may not give you truthful answers, for example they may not want to criticise the residential home they live in.

4 marks, Enquiry Skills

(e)

Use of Website

You need to show that you are aware of how to use a website effectively.

You will get one mark for saying what you would do and another for your explanation.

✓ To use the 'Elderly' website for the investigation you could use the quick search box on the page. If key words from the investigation aims were typed in here it would search the website for related information.

✓ Depending on what your hypothesis and aims are, you could click on the advertisement for the residential home to find out what it has to offer the elderly.

2. **(continued)**

HINT | In this type of question you may be asked to state advantages or disadvantages for a range of methods. You will need to know the benefits and limits of all common research methods. You will also need to understand how to use each method effectively. Methods include: interviews, Internet, surveys / questionnaires, letters, emails, libraries, newspapers, databases and observational visits.

2 marks, Enquiry Skills

SYLLABUS AREA 3 – IDEOLOGIES

QUESTION 3A – THE USA

HINT | In this section of the exam you should prepare for questions about the key concepts of **Ideology, Participation, Equality** and **Rights and Responsibilities.**

TOP EXAM TIP

Do not write your answers as lists or bullet points. Write in proper sentences.

3A. (a)

The Concept being assessed in the question is **Participation**. You have to show understanding of the concept. Answers that do not mention detailed American examples will only be awarded a maximum of five marks. You should provide detailed examples in your answer.

Each of the bullet points below makes a point and backs up the point. Any four of these bullet points would be enough to get you full marks. Open with a link to the question.

Link: Some ethnic minority citizens are more motivated to participate in politics due to;

- a more positive ethnic minority. Role models such as Barack Obama (US President), Barbara Jean Lee (member of the House of Representatives) and Ray Nagin (mayor of New Orleans) are encouraging ethnic minorities to vote.

- more Black Americans graduating from college has led to an increase of an ethnic minority "middle class" that is more likely to register and vote in elections

- some ethnic minority groups being concentrated in particular parts of the country and are therefore more likely to vote because they believe their minority candidate has a better chance of getting elected.

- education programmes that have been introduced which encourage young people to vote and participate in the political system, for example the "Citizenship Education Clearing House" and "Kids Voting in Missouri."

However some are less motivated because;

- the registration process and voting paper can be complex and difficult to complete, which is an even stronger reason not to participate if there are language problems amongst some ethnic minority groups.

- the costs involved in standing for elections are high and Black Americans and Hispanics are less able to afford this compared to other ethnic groups.

- some ethnic groups feel the political system continues to discriminate against them and that participation will not change anything.

- some ethnic minorities continue to face discrimination, with other ethnic groups refusing to vote for them.

8 marks, Knowledge and Understanding

TOP EXAM TIP

Remember you MUST use American examples in your answers to get a good mark in this section.

3A. (continued)

(b)

> In this type of question you need to give evidence to **support** and evidence to **oppose** the stated point of view. This means that Julie Smith says something which is **correct** and something which is **wrong**.
>
> For four marks you would need to do the following:
>
> To **support** – you should quote what the person says that is correct.
>
> You should then give evidence from one of the sources to show why it is correct.
>
> To **oppose** – you should quote what the person says that is wrong.
>
> You should then give evidence from one of the sources to show why it is wrong.
>
> You must clearly link the view to the sources for your support and your oppose. **If you don't make an explicit link between the views and the sources, you will only be able to get a maximum of two marks.**
>
> You must use both sources and you must use both sentences in the view to get full marks. You must also refer to other states in your evidence or you will receive a maximum of two marks.

To support
Julie Smith says that "The largest increase in voter turnout between 2000 and 2008 has been in North Carolina."

*Note that you have to compare **2000** with **2008**.*

Evidence to support
Source 1 supports this view as it shows that in 2000 the North Carolina turnout was 41% and it rose to 63% in 2008, an increase of 22% which is higher than any of the other states.

To oppose
Julie Smith says that "The highest voter turnout figures in 2008 are all to be found in the East Coast states".

Evidence to oppose
Source 2 opposes this view as it shows that although Maine and Vermont are East Coast states with higher voter turnout than any West Coast states, Washington and Oregon are higher than Florida and Jersey which are both on the East Coast.

4 marks, Enquiry Skills

> **TOP EXAM TIP**
>
> You can be asked this sort of question as support only, oppose only or support and oppose. Make sure you read the question carefully and that you understand what you are being asked to do.

> **TOP EXAM TIP**
>
> Watch the time – you have just under 30 minutes in the Credit exam for each question area.

(c)

> **Selective in the use of facts type question.**
>
> This type of question requires you to detect and explain examples of a lack of objectivity in the sources and give a developed argument when needed.
>
> Depending on the quality of your explanation, you will get up to two marks for an example of selectivity or otherwise.
>
>
>
> A good answer – one that will get the most marks, makes a direct link between the view and the sources. If you do not make **an explicit link between the view and the sources,** you will only be able to get a **maximum of four marks**.
>
> You can draw one **overall conclusion** or **conclusions to each part** of the view as to the extent of selectivity.
>
> You will receive up to two marks for the degree of selectivity; if you fail to do so, you will only get a total maximum of six out of eight possible marks.

3A. (continued)

Link: Alan Hunter's first view is "The death penalty is not an effective punishment to reduce the murder rate in the USA."

In support, source 2 shows
- A poll of police chiefs ranked the death penalty as the least effective way to reduce crime and they rated it as an inefficient way to spend taxes.

- 88% of criminologists do not believe the death penalty lowers murder rates.

In support, source 3 shows
- The South had the highest murder rate, but it accounts for over 80% of executions. The Northeast has less than 1% of all executions, but had the lowest murder rate.

Therefore, Alan Hunter is **correct** when he says that the death penalty is not an effective punishment to reduce the murder rate in the USA because police chiefs and criminologists agree with him and there is evidence from the South and Northeast that it does not work.

Link: Alan Hunter's second view is "its use is opposed by all groups within the USA."

To opppose, source 1 shows
- 64% of the American public still support capital punishment.

- Political support for capital punishment is higher than 57% for all parties

To support, source 1 shows
- Given the choice of life without parole, only 47% of the American public prefer the death penalty.

To support, source 2 shows
- Criminologists are against capital punishment.

Therefore, Alan Hunter is only **partly correct** when he says its use is opposed by all groups.

Link: Alan Hunter's third view is "There are no arguments in support of capital punishment."

To opppose, source 1 shows
- There are at least four arguments for capital punishment, including the view that it acts as a deterrant to others.

Therefore, Alan Hunter is **wrong** when he says there are no arguments in support of capital punishment.

Overall conclusion on the extent of selectivity
Alan Hunter is right in the first statement, partly right in the second and wrong in the third so he is slightly selective in the use of facts.

8 marks, Enquiry Skills

 HINT — It is a good idea to tick or cross each piece of information in the view to identify what is right and what is wrong. Don't just assume that either a sentence is right or wrong – one sentence may contain something which is true **and** something which is false.

QUESTION 3B – CHINA

 HINT — In this section of the exam you should prepare for questions about the key concepts of **Ideology, Participation, Equality** and **Rights and Responsibilities.**

3B. (a)

 The concept being assessed is **Participation**. You need to use your understanding of the concept to give detailed descriptions with relevant examples. **You must use Chinese examples** in your answer.

You should write four good points to achieve full marks in this answer.

You should start by linking to the question.

Answers could include:

One right that people have is the right to join a political party. There are several political parties in China, the biggest and main one being the Communist party. However, not all political parties are legal, such as the Chinese Democracy party. Not everyone can join the Communist party as membership is strictly controlled. In recent years however there has been a huge rise in membership, particularly among young people, to more than 75 million members.

3B. (a) **(continued)**

Another right that Chinese citizens have is the right to vote in elections at national and local level. However, they are limited in choice of candidate, as all candidates at national level have to be approved by the Communist party. At village level it is different; these elections are more likely to be 'free' and 'fair' and less likely to be absolutely controlled by the Communist party.

Another political right that is limited in China is the right to join a pressure group. While some pressure groups do exist and operate in China, such as the campaign against the Rushan nuclear power station, most pressure groups are considered to be suspicious by the Communist government in China and most pressure groups and pressure group activity is banned. An example of this is the Falungong spiritual movement.

Another political right that is limited is the right to protest and demonstrate against the government. Writing letters to newspapers or speaking out openly in the media is frowned upon and can result in arrest. People who believe in a 'Free Tibet' campaigned in March 2008 to mark the 49th anniversary of a Tibetan uprising against Chinese rule. The Chinese authorities responded with a show of force to the protests.

8 marks, Knowledge and Understanding

TOP EXAM TIP

Remember you MUST use Chinese example in your answers to get a good mark in this section.

(b)

Support and oppose type question.

In this type of question you need to give evidence to **support** and evidence to **oppose** the stated point of view. This means that Andrew Morrison says something which is correct and something which is wrong.

For four marks you would need to do the following:

To **support** – you should quote what the person says that is correct.

You should then give evidence from one of the sources to show why it is correct.

To **oppose** – you should quote what the person says that is wrong.

You should then give evidence from one of the sources to show why it is wrong.

You must clearly link the 'view' to the sources for both your statements, in support and in opposition.

You must use both sources and you must use both sentences in the view to get full marks.

To support
Andrew Morrison says that "China spends far less money than the US on its military."

Evidence to support
Source 1 supports this view as it shows that in 2007 China spent less than $200 billion on the military compared to the USA spending about $700 billion on the military in the same year.

To oppose
Andrew Morrison says that "The military priorities of China have not changed in the last twenty years."

Evidence to oppose
Source 2 opposes the view of Andrew Morrison because it says that China has changed its military priorities by reducing the number of soldiers it has and increasing spending on advanced weapons.

4 marks, Enquiry Skills

HINT

Remember when you are given a bar graph or line graph don't worry about getting the figures exactly correct. It is acceptable to say closer to, about or almost $700 billion. The actual figure was $680 billion but this is not clear in the bar graph so you wouldn't be expected to get it exactly right.

You do need to make sure that you check the unit of measurement carefully. If you say about $700 this is not correct because you have missed out the fact that the bar graph shows the information in billions.

TOP EXAM TIP

You can be asked this sort of question as support only, oppose only or support and oppose. Make sure you read the question carefully and that you understand what you are being asked to do.

3B. **(continued)**

(c)

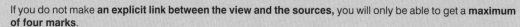

Selective in the use of facts type question.

This type of question requires you to detect and explain examples of lack of objectivity in the sources and give a developed argument when required.

You will receive up to two marks for an example of selectivity or otherwise, depending on the quality of your explanation.

For full marks, you must use all three sources.

A good answer – one that will get the most marks – makes a direct link between the view and the sources.

If you do not make **an explicit link between the view and the sources,** you will only be able to get a **maximum of four marks.**

You can draw one **overall conclusion** or **conclusions to each part** of the view as to the extent of selectivity.

You will receive up to two marks for the degree of selectivity; if you fail to do so, you will only get a total maximum of six out of eight possible marks.

The question asks 'to what extent' Mei Ling is being selective. For this you need to give conclusions about how correct or wrong you think she is. You do not need to put in the headings below but it allows you to see how you could set out such a question.

TOP EXAM TIP

Remember you MUST provide an overall conclusion or conclusions on how selective the view or statement is.

View

Mei Ling says that 'The use of the death penalty is supported by most Chinese people, especially for crimes like murder.'

Selective/not selective

- This is correct because in source 1 it shows that 58% of Chinese people agree with the death penalty.

- This is also correct because in source 1 it shows that about 80% of Chinese people agree with the use of the death penalty for murder.

Conclusion

In this statement Mei Ling has been entirely accurate in what she says. She has not been selective in her use of facts.

View

Mei Ling says that 'China only executes violent criminals.'

Selective/not selective

- This is wrong because in source 1 it says that the death penalty is used over 60 crimes including drug-trafficking, tax fraud and corruption.

- It is also wrong because source 1 says a top Government official was put to death in 2005 for taking brides.

- This is also wrong because in source 3 it says that the British man Akmal Shaikh was executed for drug-related crimes.

Conclusion

In this statement Mei Ling has been entirely wrong in what she says. She has been entirely selective in her use of facts.

View

Mei Ling says that 'Other countries like Iran use the death penalty more than China'.

Selective/not selective

- This is wrong because in source 2 it shows that Iran only executed 346 people in 2008 compared to 1,718 people in China. China executes more people than any other country listed on the map.

- However this could also be partly correct as in source 1 it says that Iran and Saudi Arabia execute more people per head of population than China.

3B. (continued)

Conclusion

In this statement Mei Ling has been partly selective in the use of facts.

View

Mei Ling says that 'China's Supreme People's Court now monitors the use of executions but they can't overturn a death sentence once it has been passed'.

Selective/not selective

- This is true for the monitoring part of this sentence as source 1 and source 3 both says that the Supreme Court monitors executions.

- However the second part of this sentence is wrong because source 1 also says that the Supreme Court can overturn executions and did so in 15% of all cases in 2007.

Conclusion

In this statement Mei Ling has been partly selective in her use of facts.

Overall conclusion

There seems to be an even split between what Mei Ling says which is true, based on the facts, and what she says which is selective in the use of the facts.

8 marks, Enquiry Skills

HINT
> It is a good idea to tick or cross each piece of information in the view to identify what is right and what is wrong. Don't just assume that either a sentence is right or wrong – one sentence may contain something which is true **and** something which is false.

SYLLABUS AREA 4 – INTERNATIONAL RELATIONS

HINT
> In this section of the exam you should prepare for questions about the key concepts of **Need** and **Power**.

4. (a)

> The concept being assessed in the question is **Power**. You have to show understanding of the concept. What powers are these 'groups' concerned about? Notice that the word 'power' is repeatedly used in the sample answer.
>
> Each of the bullet points below makes and backs up a point. Any two of these bullet points would be enough to get you full marks.
>
> Open with a link to the question.

Link: Some groups believe that the EU does not bring their country real benefits,

- As EU membership has increased, poorer countries have become members – this has diverted funding from richer countries like the UK to some of the poorer countries like Poland. Scotland now gets less regional aid than it used to as a result of this. The UK still pays a lot of money into the EU but has lost some of the power in being able to prioritise where that money is spent.

- With EU membership it is easier for workers to move from one country to another. In the past this has not been a major problem for the UK as more UK workers were working in other EU countries than the number of EU workers in the UK. Now this balance has shifted and more non-UK EU citizens are working in the UK than UK workers working in other EU countries. This causes real concerns about UK jobs being filled by foreign workers. By being in the EU the UK has lost power over who works in the UK.

- Membership of the EU can be seen as taking decision making and power away from individual countries. Some people do not like to feel that decisions are being dictated to them by other countries. The UK government has very limited control over decisions on things like immigration, fishing policy or agriculture.

4 marks, Knowledge and Understanding

HINT
> UKIP – UK Independence Party campaign for the withdrawal of the UK from the EU. Look at their website for more of their arguments against EU membership.
>
> http://www.ukip.org/content/ukip-policies/1014-campaign-policies-euro-elections-2009
>
> The Conservative Party are more wary of the benefits of the EU than the Labour or Liberal Democrat parties. However all three of these parties think that the UK should remain in the EU.

4. (continued)

(b)

> The concept being assessed in this question is **Need**. You have to show understanding of the concept in your answer. Notice that the word 'need' is used repeatedly in the answer below.
>
> Again any two of the bullet points below would be enough to get you full marks.
>
> Remember to link your answer clearly to the question.

Link: The Department for International Development (DFID) is the UK Government Department responsible for giving aid.

- In Malawi the DFID has helped meet the needs of people by providing money to build classrooms and provide equipment for schools. They have also set up teacher training schemes to help meet the educational needs of people in Malawi.

- In Uganda the DFID is helping to provide clean drinking water and better basic sanitation (toilet arrangements). This helps to meet the health needs of people in Uganda as dirty water and poor sanitation can cause the spread of diseases like cholera.

- Also in Uganda, the DFID has helped to fight the country's HIV/AIDS problem. AIDS is a major killer of people in Uganda. Although the disease cannot be cured, it can be successfully treated. The DFID has provided funding to help increase the availability of treatment. This has meant many more people can get access to Anti Retroviral Treatment (ART).

4 marks, Knowledge and Understanding

HINT

> You could look at their website for more information:
>
> http://www.dfid.gov.uk/
>
> Look at the 'Where we work' option and pick two or three African countries to find out about the work of the DFID in these places. The country profiles give you some key information about the problems in the country and how the DFID is helping.
>
> The DFID also gives money to fund the work of UN agencies, support many UK Aid charities like OXFAM and also give money to EU Aid programmes.

(c)

> **Conclusions type question.**
>
> In this type of question you need to:
>
> - make comparisons within and between the sources
>
> - make valid conclusions from the sources.
>
> - justify your conclusions using well-developed arguments
>
> A conclusion should be a trend or pattern you can see from reading the sources.
>
> In this question you need to clearly state four conclusions based on the bullet points in the question. It is best to draw a clear conclusion in one sentence and then support it with several sentences using evidence from the sources.

Answers may include:

Progress towards promoting safety in Afghanistan
There has not been good progress towards promoting safety in Afghanistan. *This is a valid conclusion.*

According to the information in source 1, NATO is committed to promoting security, stability and safety in Afghanistan.

✓ However source 3 suggests that there has not been good progress towards this because the death rates of NATO/ISAF have increased suggesting that Afghanistan is becoming less safe.

✓ In 2004 only 60 NATO/ISAF troops were killed but in 2009 this rose to over 500 troops. The figures for civilian deaths show a similar trend. In 2006 it is estimated that about 929 civilian Afghans were killed but by 2009 this figure had more than doubled.

By using this evidence you have justified your conclusion using two different sets of information from source 3 – comparing within a source.

4.   **(continued)**

Support for the Afghan Army

Many NATO countries have given a lot of support to help the Afghan National Army. *This is a valid conclusion.*

According to the information in source 1, NATO is committed to supporting the Afghan National Army (ANA).

✓   Source 1 shows that many NATO countries have provided equipment and training for the ANA. Canada has for example supplied guns and ammunition. In Source 4 it shows that many NATO countries have given large sums of money to the ANA. The UK has given 4·5 million Euros, The Netherlands 10·6 million Euros and Germany is giving 50 million Euros. These sums show strong support for the Afghan Army.

The above point also provides comparison between sources.

In this point you could also have concluded:

That many NATO countries have not been very supportive of the ANA. The evidence in source 4 shows many countries have given no money. You would need to quote figures to show this.

Or

Some NATO countries have done more that others to support the ANA financially.

Again you would use the evidence to back this up.

> **HINT** The first time you write something you should write it in full (Afghan National Army) with the abbreviation next to it (ANA). Then you can use the abbreviation of the rest of the answer.

The commitment of NATO/ISAF members to Afghanistan

1.   Some NATO countries are more committed to Afghanistan than others.

2.   The UK and the USA seem more committed to Afghanistan than many other NATO countries.

3.   Iceland and Portugal seem less committed to NATO activities in Afghanistan than other members.

Any one of these conclusions would be valid.

We will take the first conclusion listed as it is the broadest.

Some NATO countries are more committed to Afghanistan than others.

✓   Source 1 says that all members of NATO are committed to Afghanistan and that all 28 member countries have troops stationed in Afghanistan. However some countries have very few troops in the country while others have very large numbers of troops. In source 2 the USA has 34 800 troops under NATO and 36 000 in Afghanistan under another operation. The UK has 9,000 troops. When compared to Iceland, with 20 troops, and Luxembourg, with 90 troops, it is clear that some countries are more committed than others. *This provides comparison between sources.*

✓   Source 2 shows the deployment of troops within Afghanistan and source 3 shows the death rate by province. This demonstrates that some troops are being exposed to greater risk than others. UK, US and Canadian troops are stationed in some of the most dangerous areas again suggesting a higher level of commitment. *This provides comparison between sources.*

✓   Source 3 also shows that far more US troops have been killed compared to other NATO/ISAF nations. In 2009 more than 300 US troops were killed, accounting for more than half of all NATO/ISAF deaths in Afghanistan. The UK also seems to have a high death rate. In 2009 the UK lost over 100 troops compared with less than 100 for all the other NATO/ISAF countries put together if the USA is excluded.

✓   Source 4 shows that some countries are more finically committed to helping the Afghan Army than others. Germany has given by far the largest amount (50 million Euros) while a number of NATO countries have given no money to support the Afghan Army, including France and Canada.

> **HINT** This is too much to write for one conclusion. When deciding what information to use remember you need to compare between sources as part of this question so the first two points here do that better. You could still use the last two points if you have already made a number of comparisons between sources in your other conclusions.

4.   (continued)

The level of danger in different parts of Afghanistan

The South and East of Afghanistan are the most dangerous areas of the country. *This is a valid conclusion.*

✓   Source 2 shows troop deployment in Afghanistan. From this we can see that larger forces are located in the South and East of the country. In the South Region there are 36 500 troops stationed compared to 5 700 in the North Region. In the East there are 18 300 troops compared to 4 400 in the West. The high number of troops suggests these areas are more dangerous and therefore require more troops. This is supported by source 3 as it shows the number of deaths of NATO/ISAF forces in each area. The South has the highest overall death rate while the North Region has a very low death rate for NATO/ISAF troops.

This point provides comparison between sources.

8 marks, Enquiry Skills

HINT

It is a good idea to deal with each conclusion in a separate paragraph.

It is also a good idea to have a highlighter with you in the exam. You can then highlight information in the sources. This can help you pick out comparisons between sources.

TOP EXAM TIP

In all source questions you should read the sources carefully and pay attention to the headings of each source, the units of measurement (%, £, $ Millions, 100,000) and the overall trend of the sources (do the figures generally go up, down or stay the same?). Make sure that you use the information correctly.

TOP EXAM TIP

If you have time left you should check through your answers.

General Level Exam B – Worked Answers

SYLLABUS AREA 1 – LIVING IN A DEMOCRACY

HINT Remember to refer to the introduction section for more information on answering the questions.

QUESTION 1

TOP EXAM TIP

You don't need to do the whole exam paper in order. Look at the whole paper and start with the question area you think you will do best in. You should aim to keep question areas together, e.g. all of Area 3, then all of Area 1 and so on.

1. (a)

The concept being assessed here is **Representation**. This question is asking you specifically for ways that MPs work in the House of Commons. Answers that include details about what an MP does in their constituency will be given no marks.

Your answer could include two of the points detailed below. Remember, you need to explain your point and provide a relevant example. Your answer should start by linking to the question.

MPs represent their constituents by asking questions in the House of Commons about reserved issues. They could either ask the Prime Minster a question at Prime Minster's Question Time or ask a government Minister a question at Question Time. For example, an MP could ask the Prime Minister about job losses in their area and how the government plans to help people find new jobs.

MPs also represent their constituents in Parliament by proposing new laws. They can introduce Private Members' Bills about issues that affect their constituents. The MP would present their bill to Parliament who would then debate and vote on it to decide if it should become law. An example of a successful Private Members' Bill is the Fireworks Act of 2003, which imposed noise limits on fireworks and banned the use of fireworks during antisocial hours.

Other points you might choose to write about could be:

- Speaking in debates

- Participating in adjournment debate

- Joining select committees

- Discussing legislation in a committee

- Voting on laws.

4 marks, Knowledge and Understanding

HINT Remember NOT to get confused between an MP and an MSP. While some aspects of their jobs are similar, there are many differences.

TOP EXAM TIP

In this section of the exam you should prepare for questions about the key concepts of **Representation, Participation** and **Rights and Responsibilities**.

1. **(continued)**

(b)

> **Support and oppose type question.**
>
> In this type of question you need to give evidence to **support** and evidence to **oppose** the stated point of view. This means that Kevin McNeill says something which is correct and something which is wrong.
>
> For four marks you would need to do the following:
>
> To **support** – you should quote what the person says that is correct.
>
> You should then give evidence from one of the sources to show why it is correct.
>
> To **oppose** – you should quote what the person says that is wrong.
>
> You should then give evidence from one of the sources to show why it is wrong.
>
> You must clearly link the 'view' to the sources for both your statements, in support and in opposition. If you don't make a clear link between the views and the sources, you will only receive a maximum of two marks.
>
> You must use both sources and you must use both sentences in the view to get full marks.

Kevin McNeill says, "Men make up the majority of trade union membership."

Evidence to support this view

This is true because source 1 shows that out of the five trade unions mentioned, all have a higher male membership than female.

Kevin McNeill says "The main reason why women join a trade union is to negotiate better pay."

Evidence to oppose this view

Source 2 shows us that 46% of women join a union to negotiate better working conditions such as more holidays or improved health and safety, whereas only 21% of women join a union to negotiate better pay.

4 marks, Enquiry Skills

> **TOP EXAM TIP**
>
> You can be asked this sort of question as support only, oppose only or support and oppose. Make sure you read the question carefully and that you understand what you are being asked to do.

> **TOP EXAM TIP**
>
> Watch the time – you only have about 20 minutes in the General exam for each question area.

(c)

> The concept being assessed here is **Participation**. Make sure you specifically write about the methods that pressure groups use when campaigning. Your answer should start by linking to the question.

One right that a pressure group has when campaigning is to organise a protest march or demonstration. Another right a pressure group has is to organise a petition.

The responsibility that goes along with the right to organise a protest march or demonstration is to make sure the police are notified beforehand and to make sure the demonstration is free from violence and that people do not break the law.

4 marks, Knowledge and Understanding

> HINT > Nationally, pupils in Modern Studies usually do less well in their Knowledge and Understanding answers. You must make sure you revise all sections thoroughly.

(d)

> **Conclusions type question.**
>
> A conclusion should be a trend or pattern you can see from reading the sources.
>
> In this question you need to clearly state two conclusions based on the bullet points in the question. It is best to have a clear conclusion in one sentence and then a second sentence using evidence from the sources to support your conclusion.

Answers may include:

Conclusion
*   The party with the biggest change in the occupation of their MPs was the Labour Party.

1. (continued)

Evidence
- The number of MPs who came from a professional background in the Labour party significantly decreased between 1997 and 2005 with 225 of their MPs coming from a professional background in 1997 compared to only 141 in 2005.

Conclusion
- As the total number of MPs rises for each political party, the number of women and ethnic minority MPs increases for most political parties.

Evidence
- The Conservatives increased their MPs in 2005 to 198 and, at the same time, the number of women MPs for the Conservative Party increased to 17 and the number of ethnic minority MPs increased to 2.

4 marks, Enquiry Skills

HINT

It is a good idea to deal with each conclusion in a separate paragraph.

It is also a good idea to have a highlighter with you in the exam. You can then highlight information in the sources. This can help you pick out comparisons between sources.

TOP EXAM TIP

Remember to make sure you give clear conclusions.

SYLLABUS AREA 2 – CHANGING SOCIETY

QUESTION 2

HINT

In this section of the exam you should prepare for questions about the key concepts of **Ideology**, **Equality** and **Need**.

2. (a)

The concept being assessed in this question is **Need**. You need to give detailed descriptions to get full marks. Make sure you write about residential homes and not other types of homes as sometimes it can be easy to become confused.

Remember to link your answer clearly to the question.

One way that residential homes can help meet the needs of the elderly is by providing meals so that they can get the nutrition they need to keep healthy.

Another way that residential homes can help meet the needs of the elderly is by having communal areas for residents where they can socialise. Sometimes these areas can have entertainment and games events to keep elderly people mentally alert.

4 marks, Knowledge and Understanding

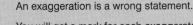

TOP EXAM TIP

Read all the questions carefully – make sure you understand what you are being asked.

(b)

In this type of question you have to detect and explain exaggeration.

An exaggeration is a wrong statement.

You will get a mark for each exaggerated statement you correctly identify – you should repeat the exaggeration stating clearly that it is exaggerated.

You will then get another mark for providing evidence to prove it is an exaggerated statement.

Exaggerated statement
The first exaggerated statement by Richard Duncan is when he says "no disabled workers have been helped into work through the New Deal"

Evidence
Richard is wrong because source 1 says 61% of disabled workers have found work as a result of the New Deal.

2.   (continued)

Exaggerated statement

The second exaggerated statement from Richard Duncan is that "most people found shop work following the New Deal."

Evidence

Richard is wrong because source 2 shows that 24% of people found shop work, but 28% found unskilled factory work.

The easiest way to do this type of question is to look at each of the statements or views expressed by the person. For each statement or view tick or cross on your exam paper to say whether it is correct or wrong based on the table, bar graph or written source you have been given. Check all the statements as this will help you select the two exaggerated ones.

Remember when you are given a bar graph or line graph, do not worry about getting the figures exactly correct. It is acceptable to say 'about' or 'almost' 24%. The actual figure in shop work was 24% but this is not clear in the bar graph so you would not be expected to get the figure exactly right. You do need to make sure that you check the unit of measurement carefully. If you say about 24 people this is not correct because you have missed out the fact that the bar graph shows the information in percentages.

4 marks, Enquiry Skills

TOP EXAM TIP

Remember exaggeration means there is something incorrect in the statement.

(c)

The concept is **Equality**. You need to provide detailed explanations to get full marks. Your answer should start by linking to the question.

Some elderly people have better health than others. Some elderly people live in poorer quality houses which can lead to health problems such as respiratory and cardiovascular disease, asthma, and arthritis.

Wealth is another reason why some elderly people have better health than others. Wealthy elderly people are able to afford private health care, which can sometimes mean that they get operations sooner than others.

4 marks, Knowledge and Understanding

(d)

In this type of question you need to correctly identify two different points of view. The concept is **Equality**. You will get two marks for each difference you correctly identify – you must quote views from both sources for each difference you identify. In this question you need to show two differences.

Difference 1

Source 1 says that the development of technology can only lead to more successful companies.

Source 2 says the rate at which new technology is developing will lead to more companies failing.

Difference 2

Source 1 says that more jobs will be created which will bring down unemployment rates.

Source 2 says that the rate of development of new technology will lead to a loss of jobs and rising unemployment.

4 marks, Enquiry Skills

TOP EXAM TIP

Remember you must quote from both sources to show a difference.

SYLLABUS AREA 3 – IDEOLOGIES USA OR CHINA

HINT   In this section of the exam you should prepare for questions about the key concepts of **Ideology**, **Participation**, **Equality** and **Rights and Responsibilities**.

TOP EXAM TIP

Do not write your answers as lists or bullet points. Write in proper sentences.

QUESTION 3A – THE USA

3A. *(a)*

> HINT
>
> The concept being assessed in this question is **Ideology**. You have to show understanding of the concept. Two descriptions are required for full marks. **If you do not give an American example, you will only receive a maximum of three marks.**
>
> Each of the bullet points below makes a point and backs up the point. Two of these bullet points would be enough to get you full marks. Open with a link to the question.

Link: More ethnic minorities have started up their own businesses because:

- It is part of the American Dream. Ethnic minorities have seen role models become rich by working hard and making a success of their business, e.g. Sean "Puffy" Combs (P. Diddy), with his music and his clothing line, Sean John, and Oprah Winfrey, with her company Harpo Inc.

- Some ethnic minorities face prejudice and discrimination in the employment market and starting a business is a means of overcoming this problem.

You could also add the more general points:

- America is a capitalist country and people are encouraged to start their own businesses.

- Taxes are low meaning that people can keep most of the profits they make.

4 marks, Knowledge and Understanding

> **TOP EXAM TIP**
>
> Remember you MUST use American examples in your answers to get a good mark in this section.

(b)

> **Support and oppose type question.**
>
> In this type of question you need to give evidence to **support** and evidence to **oppose** the stated point of view. This means that Keir Martin says something which is correct and something which is wrong.
>
> For four marks you would need to do the following:
>
> To **support** – you should quote what the person says that is correct.
>
> You should then give evidence from one of the sources to show why it is correct.
>
> To **oppose** – you should quote what the person says that is wrong.
>
> You should then give evidence from one of the sources to show why it is wrong.
>
> You must clearly link the 'view' to the sources for both your statements, in support and in opposition. If you don't make a clear link between the views and the sources, you will only receive a maximum of two marks.
>
> You must use both sources and you must use both sentences in the view to get full marks.

To support
Keir Martin says that "In the 2008 Presidential election, the winner had a clear majority."

Evidence to support
Source 1 supports this view as it shows Obama received 54% and McCain only 46%, which is a clear majority.

To oppose
Keir Martin says that "The winner also received more votes than his opponent in all age ranges."

Evidence to oppose
Source 2 opposes this view as it shows that although Obama received more votes than McCain in most age ranges, more votes were received by McCain in the 65+ age range.

4 marks, Enquiry Skills

> **TOP EXAM TIP**
>
> You can be asked this sort of question as support only, oppose only or support and oppose. Make sure you read the question carefully and that you understand what you are being asked to do.

3A. (continued)

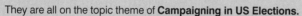

TOP EXAM TIP

Watch the time – you only have about 20 minutes in the General exam for each question area.

(*c*), (*d*) and (*e*)

Investigating questions.

Questions **3A.** (*c*), (*d*) and (*e*) below are an investigating set of questions.

They are all on the topic theme of **Campaigning in US Elections.**

Look out for the man with a question mark in his head – he shows you that this is an investigating set of questions.

(*c*)

Aims.

In this question, you need to give relevant aims for an investigative topic.

Depending on the quality and relevance of your answer, one mark will be awarded for each aim.

You need to give two aims in order to get full marks.

Your aims are what you would need to find out to complete your investigation. It is a good idea to start each aim 'To find out..........' as shown below.

These aims would not get any marks as they are too basic:

- to find out about US elections
- to find out about campaigning.

These aims would get 1 mark each:

- to find out about the methods used to campaign in US elections
- to find out how much money is spent on US election campaigns
- to find out about the people who stand in election campaigns
- to find out what party workers do to help with US election campaigns.

You may be able to think of some other aims.

2 marks, Enquiry Skills

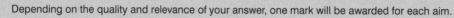

TOP EXAM TIP

Check that your aims relate to the topic you have been given and try and include reference to a concept, e.g. **Representation**.

(*d*)

Advantage and disadvantage.

In this type of question you need to give one advantage and one disadvantage.

You will get one mark for a correct advantage of sending a letter and one mark for a correct disadvantage.

Answers may include:

Advantage *(any one point would do)*
- You can spend time making sure your questions are well worded.
- It is cheap and easy to send.
- If you use the person's name, you are more likely to get a response.

Disadvantage *(any one point would do)*
- You might get a reply that does not really answer what you needed to know.
- You might not get an answer – perhaps the person is too busy.
- You need to keep your letter short and you might not be able to include as much detail as you need.

2 marks, Enquiry Skills

HINT

In this type of question you may be asked to state advantages or disadvantages for a range of methods. You will need to know the benefits and limits of all common research methods. You will also need to understand how to use each method effectively. Methods include: interviews, Internet, surveys/questionnaires, letters, emails, libraries, newspapers, databases and observational visits.

3A. (continued)

(e)

> **Use of Website.**
>
> You will receive one mark for each correct way and one mark for each correct explanation of why the website is good. You must give two methods for full marks. Any of the answers below would each receive two marks.

- Use the search facility to find a particular representative's website. This would be good because you could then find out their contact details to ask questions about their election campaign.

- You could click on the education resources and look for information on election campaigns.

- You could use the search facility and type in "election campaigns" to see all the relevant information on the site.

4 marks, Enquiry Skills

HINT | In this section of the exam you should prepare for questions about the key concepts of **Ideology**, **Participation**, **Equality** and **Rights and Responsibilities**.

TOP EXAM TIP

Do not write your answers as lists or bullet points. Write in proper sentences.

QUESTION 3B – CHINA

3B. (a)

> The concept being assessed is **Participation**. You need to provide detailed descriptions to get full marks. You should try to write two good, detailed points. In your answer **you must use Chinese examples**. Your answer should start by linking to the question.

You might write that:

Chinese citizens can participate in politics by being able to joining the Communist party. By becoming a member of the Communist party you have more of a say in how the party is run and might be able to contribute to decision making.

Chinese citizens can also participate in some elections by voting. For example Chinese citizens can vote in village elections to decide who is going to govern them at a local level.

4 marks, Knowledge and Understanding

TOP EXAM TIP

Remember you MUST use Chinese examples in your answers to get a good mark in this section.

(b)

> **Support and oppose type question.**
>
> In this type of question you need to give evidence to **support** and evidence to **oppose** the stated point of view. This means that Rachel Bennie says something which is correct and something which is wrong.
>
> For four marks you would need to do the following:
>
> To **support** – you should quote what the person says that is correct.
>
> You should then give evidence from one of the sources to show why it is correct.
>
> To **oppose** – you should quote what the person says that is wrong.
>
> You should then give evidence from one of the sources to show why it is wrong.
>
> You must clearly link the 'view' to the sources for both your statements, in support and in opposition. If you don't make a clear link between the views and the sources, you will only receive a maximum of two marks.
>
> You must use both sources and you must use both sentences in the view to get full marks.

To support
- Rachel Bennie says, "China has recently overtaken the USA in CO_2 pollution."

Evidence to support
- Source 1 supports this view as it shows that in 2006 China overtook the USA in CO_2 emissions with closer to 6,500 million tons compared to almost 5,500 million tons for the USA.

3B. (continued)

To oppose

Rachel Bennie says, "between 1960 and 2005 China is the fourth worst country for cumulative CO_2 emissions in the world."

Evidence to oppose

Source 2 opposes this part of the view as it shows that China is the second biggest contributor to CO_2 emissions over this time period with 11% of all CO_2 emissions compared to Germany and Japan who are in joint fourth place with 5% of CO_2 emissions.

4 marks, Enquiry Skills

> *HINT*
>
> You don't have worry about the exact figures in a line graph – it is OK to say closer to 6,500 million tons or about 6,500 million tons. However you need to make sure that you check the unit of measurement carefully. If you say about 6,500 tons this is not correct because you have missed out the fact that the line graph shows the information in millions of tons.

> **TOP EXAM TIP**
>
> Watch the time – you only have about 20 minutes in the General exam for each question area.

> **TOP EXAM TIP**
>
> You can be asked this sort of question as support only, oppose only or support and oppose. Make sure you read the question carefully and that you understand what you are being asked to do.

(c), (d) and (e)

> **Investigating questions**
>
> Questions **3B.** (c), (d) and (e) below are an investigating set of questions.
>
> They are all on the topic theme of **Freedom of information in China.**
>
> Look out for the man with the question mark in his head – he shows you this is an investigating set of questions.

(c)

> **Aims.**
>
> In this question, you need to give relevant aims for an investigative topic.
>
> Depending on the quality and relevance of your answer, one mark will be awarded for each aim.
>
> You need to give two aims in order to get full marks.
>
> Your aims are what you would need to find out to complete your investigation. It is a good idea to start each aim 'To find out..........' as shown below.

These aims would not get any marks as they are too basic:

- to find out about freedom
- to find out about China.

These aims would get 1 mark each:

- to find out about freedom to access the internet in China
- to find out what freedom newspapers and television have in China
- to find out about the freedom to protest against the government in China
- to find out whether freedom of information has increased in China.

You may be able to think of some other aims.

2 marks, Enquiry Skills

> **TOP EXAM TIP**
>
> Check that your aims relate to the topic you have been given and try and include reference to a concept e.g. **Representation.**

3B. **(continued)**

(d)

> **Choose and justify methods.**
>
> In this type of question you need to choose two appropriate methods of enquiry.
>
> For each method you need to explain why it is a good method to get information to help you with your investigation.
>
> You will get one mark for each correct method and one mark for each correct reason.

Answers may include:

Method
Using the internet

Reason *(any one point would do)*
- An organisation like Amnesty International will have their own website and this could be used to access their reports on the issue of freedoms in China.

- Information on the websites of large organisation will usually be updated fairly regularly so you should find current information.

- The internet gives quick and cheap access to lots of information about groups like Amnesty International.

Method
Using email.

Reason *(any one point would do)*
- This allows you to ask for specific information which you need for your investigation.

- Sending an email is a quick method of contacting a group like Amnesty International.

4 marks, Enquiry Skills

> HINT
>
> You could use the first reason for email if you had instead decided to write a letter. Email is a faster method than writing a letter so the second point would not be as good a justification for a letter.

(e)

> **Advantage and disadvantage**
>
> In this type of question you need to give one advantage and one disadvantage.
> In this case you have been given information about a TV programme.

Advantage *(any one point would do)*
- This programme is relevant to the topic as it looks at the freedom of the media.

- This programme is still fairly up to date as it was first shown in the summer of 2008.

Disadvantage *(any one point would do)*
- This programme only looks at the foreign media and does not tell us about the Chinese media.

- The information about the programme says it is about the freedom of the media so it may not look at freedoms such as the freedom to protest.

- The information says that the Chinese Government promised more freedom in the run up to the 2008 Olympics but this does not guarantee that any of these freedoms continued after the Olympics so in this way the programme could be out of date.

2 marks, Enquiry Skills

> HINT
>
> In this type of question you may be asked to state advantages or disadvantages for a range of methods. You will need to know the benefits and limits of all common research methods. You will also need to understand how to use each method effectively. Methods include: interviews, Internet, surveys/ questionnaires, letters, emails, libraries, newspapers, databases and observational visits.

SYLLABUS AREA 4 – INTERNATIONAL RELATIONS

HINT In this section of the exam you should prepare for questions about the key concepts of **Need** and **Power**.

TOP EXAM TIP

You don't need to do the whole exam paper in order. Look at the whole paper and start with the question area you think you will do best in. You should aim to keep question areas together, e.g. all of Area 3, then all of Area 1 and so on.

QUESTION 4

4. (*a*) Describe, in detail, the ways in which NATO membership continues to meet the needs of member countries.

The main concept is **Need**. You must link your answer to this concept. Notice that the word 'need' is repeatedly used in the sample answer below.

You should describe clearly with examples of how NATO meets the needs of member countries.

You can get up to three marks for each individual point, depending on how well you describe and explain it. Usually in a four mark question it is easier to make two points and explain each of them well.

Open with a link to the question.

Any two of the sections below would be enough to get full marks.

Link: NATO continues to provide benefits to member counties:

Collective security: Being in any sort of alliance means that you have safety in numbers. You have other countries that are going to support and help you if you come under attack. This should make a country feel safer, thus meeting a need. After the 2001 terrorist attacks on the USA NATO countries responded with offers of help to the USA. This included some NATO members joining the USA in the invasion of Afghanistan as the Government there had helped Al Qaeda terrorists.

Shared costs of defence: Having the best and most up to date weapons and training can be very expensive. Being part of a military alliance allows for some of these costs to be shared and therefore reduced. Not all countries in NATO have nuclear weapons but they are protected by the other members who do have these weapons. This again meets a need to have cost-effective defence.

Working together: The troops in Afghanistan are under the command of NATO. This means that all the countries with troops in Afghanistan, such as the UK, USA and Germany, are able to work together to better meet the needs of all the countries involved.

4 marks, Knowledge and Understanding

(*b*)

In this type of question you have to detect and explain exaggeration.

An exaggeration is a wrong statement.

You will get a mark for each exaggerated statement you correctly identify – you should repeat the exaggeration stating clearly that it is exaggerated.

You will then get another mark for providing evidence to prove it is an exaggerated statement.

Exaggerated statement
The first exaggerated statement by James Douglas is when he says "Very few people live in poverty in Malawi."

Evidence
James is wrong because source 1 says 40% of people in Malawi live in poverty. This is not a few people but a large percentage.

Exaggerated statement
The second exaggerated statement form James Douglas is that "DFID spent more money on Malawi in 2007/08 than on any other African country."

Evidence
James is wrong because source 2 is clear that the DFID spent more money in Sudan, with over £60 million pounds being spent. About £2 million was spent on Malawi.

4 marks, Enquiry Skills

4. **(continued)**

HINT > The easiest way to do this type of question is to look at each of the statements or views expressed by the person. For each statement or view tick or cross on your exam paper to say whether it is correct or wrong based on the table, bar graph or written source you have been given. Check all the statements as this will help you make sure you have the selected the two exaggerated ones.

TOP EXAM TIP

Remember exaggeration means there is something incorrect in the statement.

(c)

It is easier to answer this question if you use the clues in the boxes. You could get full marks if you explained both in detail.

In this question the concept is **Power**. You must show that you understand the power that Aid gives the developed (rich) countries over the developing (poor) countries. Notice that the word 'power' is repeatedly used in the sample answer below.

Link: Developed countries have different reasons for giving support to developing countries.

Voting in the UN: Developed countries tend to give aid to developing countries that are supportive of their ideas. This can be seen in voting in the UN. This increases the power and influence of developed countries. Countries that support the UK in UN votes, on issues like the situations in Iraq or Afghanistan or on other international concerns, are more likely to get aid from the UK.

Tied Aid: The UK has officially ended the use of Tied Aid but many other developed countries still use it. Tied Aid is when a developed country places conditions on the aid it gives to developing countries. An example of this would be when a country says it will give money to an African country to buy drug treatments but that they must buy the drugs from drug companies owned by the country even if they do not offer the best price. This means that much of the Aid money actually comes back to the donor country. This shows the power of the richer countries over the poorer ones.

4 marks, Knowledge and Understanding

HINT > You could still get full marks without using the boxes if you gave other examples. For example – military support – developing countries letting developed countries use their airports to refuel military aircraft.

(d)

This is an 'Option choice' type of question where you need to make a clear choice. To get full marks in your answer you need find two pieces of evidence to support your choice and you need to link your evidence about the programme clearly to the background information.

Answers that do not make a clear link between the project choice and the Background information can only get a maximum of two marks out of four. You must remember to link!

Correct responses include:

I choose Project A – Gaelic Writing Skills
This would be the best choice for a number of reasons.

✓ This project will improve the Gaelic writing skills of journalists and writers. This can be linked to the priority to protect and support the Gaelic language.

✓ The project is going to use online learning to reach people in even the remotest parts of the area. This links to the priority to ensure that everyone has good access to education.

✓ The project is using online learning so it will not be adding to car pollution by requiring people to travel to take part in the course. This links to the priority to protect the local environment by such measures as reducing car pollution.

I choose Project B – Hospitality Training
This would be the best choice for a number of reasons.

✓ This project will provide training to improve skills. This links to the priority to help people find suitable training.

✓ The project will hopefully increase tourism in the area. This links to the priority to help people to stay in the Highlands and Islands as more jobs will be available.

✓ This project will also provide training in Polish. This would link to the priority to ensure that certain groups are not discriminated against.

4. **(continued)**

To get full marks any two sets of points from Project A or B would do.

The answers on the previous page have been set out with two sentences for each point. The first sentence refers to the project information. The second sentence links it to the background information. This is the best way to set out your answer.

4 marks, Enquiry Skills

HINT

In this type of question don't waste time trying to decide which option is the best. There is no right or wrong option. Either project could be chosen as there is enough information to support both. In fact in this case both projects are real projects approved for EU funding so you could use the information in a KU answer. It is how you support your choice and how you link it to the background information that gets you the marks.

TOP EXAM TIP

In this type of question there is always enough evidence to support either choice.

TOP EXAM TIP

If you have time left you should check through your answers.

SYLLABUS AREA 1 – LIVING IN A DEMOCRACY

> **HINT** Remember to refer to the introduction section for more information on answering the questions.

> **TOP EXAM TIP**
> You don't need to do the whole exam paper in order. Look at the whole paper and start with the question area you think you will do best in. You should aim to keep question areas together, e.g. all of Area 3, then all of Area 1 and so on.

QUESTION 1

1. (a)

> The concept being assessed is **Rights and Responsibilities**. You need to show an understanding of the concept and provide full, detailed explanations to get full marks. You should start by linking to the question.
>
> Any two of the paragraphs below would be enough for full marks.

Trade unions have the right to ballot their members on whether they should take industrial action in a dispute. They have the responsibility to make sure this ballot is carried out in secret and that no trade union member faces intimidation and is forced into voting a certain way.

Another right that trade unions have is to represent their members' views by asking the management questions about wages and working conditions and to take up grievances on behalf of their members. They have the responsibility to make sure they do not threaten people or behave in an unreasonable way by demanding conditions that the company is not able to deliver.

Another right that trade unions have is to recruit new members into the union to increase its membership and increase its bargaining position within the company. However they cannot force people to join a union. They have the responsibility to respect the wishes of people who may not wish to join and cannot bully them or make them feel uncomfortable in their working environment.

6 marks, Knowledge and Understanding

> **HINT** Nationally pupils in Modern Studies usually do less well in their Knowledge and Understanding answers. You must make sure you revise all sections thoroughly.

> **TOP EXAM TIP**
> In this section of the exam you should prepare for questions about the key concepts of **Representation**, **Participation** and **Rights and Responsibilities**.

(b)

> The concept being assessed is **Participation**. You need to show an understanding of the concept and provide full, detailed explanations to get full marks. You should start by linking to the question.

Pressure groups can influence elected representatives in a variety of ways. One way they can influence elected representatives is by organising a mass letter-writing campaign. This would involve members of the pressure group each sending a letter to either their local representative or maybe a government minister or even the Prime Minister. They might even write letters to national newspapers aimed at publicising their campaign further. For example, during the Iraq war, several pressure groups were involved in an anti-war campaign. Writing letters to elected representatives shows the scale of support for a particular cause.

Another way that pressure groups can influence elected representatives is by organising petitions (a petition is a collection of signatures of people who support their cause). Having thousands of signatures sends a clear signal to elected representatives that there is much support for a particular cause, making it more likely that the representatives will take action. For example, members of Amnesty International organised online petitions when the British man, Akmal Shaikh, who suffered from a mental illness, was sentenced in death in China in December 2009.

4 marks, Knowledge and Understanding

> **TOP EXAM TIP**
> Watch the time – you have just under 30 minutes in the Credit exam for each question area.

1.   (continued)

(c)

> **Selective in the use of facts type question.**
>
> This type of question requires you to detect and explain examples of a lack of objectivity in the sources and give a developed argument when needed.
>
> Depending on the quality of your explanation, you will get up to two marks for an example of selectivity or otherwise.
>
> For full marks, you must use all three sources.
>
> A good answer, one that will get the most marks, makes a direct link between the view and the sources.
>
> If you do not make **an explicit link between the view and the sources,** you will only be able to get a **maximum of four marks.**
>
> You can draw one **overall conclusion** or **conclusions to each part** of the view as to the extent of selectivity.
>
> You will receive up to two marks for the degree of selectivity; if you fail to do so, you will only get a total maximum of six out of eight possible marks.

Kate Wilson says that "Young white men are the most likely group to be involved in disruptive methods when participating in pressure group activity." This is partly correct as source 1 shows that in the recent demonstration by the 'Justice for all' pressure group, most of the arrests were of young men. This is supported in source 2 where it shows that men are more likely to be involved in direct action than women. This is further supported by looking at the table of the percentage of people involved in direct action which shows that white men are more likely to be involved in direct action than men from all other ethnic groups. However, the view is not correct when it says they are the most likely group to be involved as the graph in source 2 shows that there are more white women involved in direct action than white men. *As this paragraph clearly concludes the question, it would be awarded a maximum of* **3 marks**.

"'Justice for all' caused major disruption to the roads and transport network at the G8 Summit" is partly correct as source 3 clearly shows that many roads had to be closed around the Westminster area. However the disruption was not 'major', only 'minimal' as stated in source 1. It was also not as much as the disruption caused by other pressure groups such as the 'FREE GAZA' group. Therefore Kate Wilson is only being slightly selective.
This also answers the part of the question about the extent of Kate Wilson being selective – **2 marks**.

"Damage to the UK economy is the biggest impact of Pressure Group activity" is mostly true and Kate Wilson therefore is not being selective in her use of facts. The actions of 'Justice for all' caused several millions of pounds worth of damage and lost business. Source 1 shows that property was damaged and the windows of several businesses were smashed. This is supported in source 2, which shows that this one pressure group caused damage to cars, buses, property and lost business totalling more than £3 million. In addition to that the cost of the police operation to protect the public and the protesters cost £2·7 million therefore Kate is correct when she says that damage to the UK economy is the biggest impact of pressure group activity. *This also answers the part of the question about the extent of Kate Wilson being selective –* **2 marks**.

You now have to weigh up the extent of the selectivity. If two statements were selective and one isn't then you would say that Kate Wilson was being very selective in her use of facts. If only one out of the three statements were selective then you could say that Kate Wilson was being slightly selective.

Overall therefore Kate Wilson is being slightly selective in her use of facts as one out of the three statements is incorrect and only part of the first sentence is correct – **2 marks**.

8 marks, Enquiry Skills

HINT   It is a good idea to tick or cross each piece of information in the view to identify what is right and what is wrong. Don't just assume that either a sentence is right or wrong – one sentence may contain something which is true **and** something which is false.

TOP EXAM TIP

Remember you MUST provide an overall conclusion or conclusions on how selective the view or statement is.

SYLLABUS AREA 2 – CHANGING SOCIETY

TOP EXAM TIP

Do not write your answers as lists or bullet points. Write in proper sentences.

The concept being assessed is **Ideology**. You need to use your understanding of the concept to give detailed descriptions with relevant examples. Aim to write three good points for six marks. You should aim to link the service provided with the need that is being met. You should start by linking to the question.

QUESTION 2

2. (a) <u>National Government</u>

- Meets financial needs by providing a State pension (to all women over 60 and all men over 65) and other benefits such as the winter fuel allowance. It also provides a carer allowance for people who look after the elderly.

- Meets health needs by providing the National Health Service, which provides access to GPs, free prescriptions, outpatient services and operations.

- In Scotland the Scottish Parliament provides free personal care for the elderly, which means that elderly people can get help with personal hygiene, e.g. help bathing and hair washing. It might also include counseling and support for bereavement management. Personal support can also help with personal assistance such as help with getting dressed, getting up and going to bed and help with surgical appliances.

<u>Local Councils</u>

- Meet health needs of the elderly by providing community care, which allows elderly people to remain in their home. A social worker is assigned to assess the needs of the elderly person and devise a care plan to help them.

- Meet housing needs by providing services to adapt existing home, e.g. install stair lifts. Local councils also provide sheltered housing which provide an elderly person with their own flat but with a 24-hour warden on site and a communal area to meet with other elderly people. Local councils can also provide residential and nursing homes in the local area for elderly people that require more care.

- Local councils can also provide day centres and lunch clubs which allow elderly people to get out and socialise with other elderly people to stop them from becoming lonely.

6 marks, Knowledge and Understanding

HINT　　In this section of the exam you should prepare for questions about the key concepts of **Ideology**, **Equality** and **Need**.

(b)

Support and oppose type question.

In this type of question you need to give evidence to **support** and evidence to **oppose** the stated point of view. This means that Andrew Goldie says something which is correct and something which is wrong.

For four marks you would need to do the following:

To **support** – you should quote what the person says that is correct.

You should then give evidence from one of the sources to show why it is correct.

To **oppose** – you should quote what the person says that is wrong.

You should then give evidence from one of the sources to show why it is wrong.

You must clearly link the 'view' to the sources for both your statements, in support and in opposition. If you don't make a clear link between the views and the sources, you will only receive a maximum of two marks.

You must use both sources and you must use both sentences in the view to get full marks.

To support

Andrew Goldie says that "The local authority with the biggest % difference between elderly people aged 65+ and 65–84 also had the biggest increase in cost of care for elderly services."

Evidence to support

Source 1 supports this view as it shows that Dumfries & Galloway had 19% of elderly people aged 65+ and 16% aged 65–84, a difference of 3% which is bigger than any other authority. Dumfries & Galloway had an increase in costs of £800 000 which was also more than any other authority. *(Note that the amount of money in source 1 is in £000s)*

2. **(continued)**

To oppose

Andrew Goldie says that "The local authority with the smallest increase in cost of care was Stirling."

Evidence to oppose

Source 2 opposes this view as it shows that Argyll & Bute's costs increased by £400 000, but Highland increased by £300 000, which is smaller than Argyll & Bute's.

4 marks, Enquiry Skills

HINT

When you are given a bar graph or line graph, do not worry about getting the figures exactly correct. It is acceptable to say about or almost 19% aged 65+. The actual percentage was 19% but this might not be clear in the bar graph so you would not be expected to get it exactly right.

In source 2, make sure that you check the unit of measurement carefully. If you say Argyll & Bute's costs increased by £400 this is not correct because you have missed out the fact that the bar graph shows the information in £000s.

TOP EXAM TIP

Read all the questions carefully – make sure you understand what you are being asked.

(c)

Conclusions type question.

In this type of question you need to:

- make comparisons within and between the sources

- make valid conclusions from the sources

- justify your conclusions using well-developed arguments.

A conclusion should be a trend or pattern you can see from reading the sources.

In this question you need to clearly state four conclusions based on the bullet points in the question. It is best to draw a clear conclusion in one sentence and then support it with several sentences using evidence from the sources.

The relationship between occupation and owner-occupied housing.

Using source 1 and source 4, it is clear that the wards with the highest percentage of managers tend to have a higher percentage of owner occupied housing.

For example, Hillhead, Partick and Langside have the highest % of managers and also have the highest % of owner occupiers.

The relationship between life expectancy and employment.

Using source 2 and source 3, it is clear that the wards with the lowest rate of employment tend to have lower life expectancy.

For example, Calton has the lowest employment with only 44·7% and the lowest life expectancy of 74·6 years for females and only 61·9 for males.

The electoral ward whose employment statistics are most like that of Glasgow as a whole.

Using "Focus on Glasgow" and source 3, it is clear that Linn's employment statistics are most like Glasgow as a whole.

It is closest to the Glasgow % in three areas (benefits claimants, on incapacity benefit and in employment) and second closest for the fourth area (on income support).

The electoral ward that would be most desirable to live in.

Langside would be most desirable.

It has the highest employment rate and the second-highest life expectancy for males and females.

8 marks, Enquiry Skills

HINT

It is a good idea to deal with each conclusion in a separate paragraph.

It is also a good idea to have a highlighter with you in the exam. You can then highlight information in the sources. This can help you pick out comparisons between sources.

TOP EXAM TIP

Remember to make sure you give clear conclusions.

SYLLABUS AREA 3 – IDEOLOGIES

QUESTION 3A – THE USA

HINT

In this section of the exam you should prepare for questions about the key concepts of **Ideology**, **Participation**, **Equality** and **Rights and Responsibilities**.

TOP EXAM TIP

Do not write your answers as lists or bullet points. Write in proper sentences.

3A. *(a)*

The Concept being assessed in the question is **Equality**. You have to show understanding of the concept in your answer. Answers that **do not mention detailed American** examples will only be able to get a **maximum of five marks**. You should provide detailed examples with your answer.

Each of the bullet points below makes a point and backs up the point. Four of these bullet points would be enough to get you full marks. Make sure you discuss economic **and** social areas. Open with a link to the question.

Link: Social inequalities exist in areas such as

Education
- Some Americans attend high quality schools with excellent resources whilst others attend run down schools with few resources and poorer standards of education. Hispanics and Black Americans are less likely than Asians and Whites to complete their education, with Hispanics being the most likely of all groups to drop out of school early.

Health
- Some groups can afford private health insurance and receive high quality care, whilst others cannot and instead have to rely on the State through Medicare and Medicaid which provides less high quality care. Black Americans and Hispanics are least likely to have private insurance.

Housing
- Wealthy people tend to live in the suburbs where they can afford houses that are of better quality. Black Americans and Hispanics are more likely than whites to live in the more run-down inner city areas (ghetto areas) where housing can be very poor.

Link: Economic inequalities exist in areas such as

Employment/Unemployment
- Some ethnic groups are less likely than others to find employment because of their poorer qualifications and possibly discrimination. Asians and Whites are the ethnic groups most likely to be employed, whilst Black Americans and Hispanics are the least likely to be in work.

Wealth/Poverty
- Black Americans and Hispanics tend to receive lower levels of pay compared to Whites and Asians which means that even if they are in employment, they experience a poorer standard of living.

Prejudice and Discrimination (relevant to social and economic)
- Discrimination on the basis of race, gender, religion and nationality can lead to inequalities in all of the above social and economic areas. Ethnic minorities tend to do less well in all of the above areas.

8 marks, Knowledge and Understanding

TOP EXAM TIP

Remember you MUST use American examples in your answers to get a good mark in this section.

(b)

Decision Making

In your answer, you need to make a clear choice.

To get full marks in this answer you again need to use all the information. Your answers must make explicit links between the background information about health care in America and Sources 1 and 2.

You are asked to choose who you most agree with. There is no right or wrong answer as the evidence supports both views. What matters is how you use the information to support your choice and how you reason your rejection of the other person.

You should clearly link your choice to the information about health care.

The following answers have been set out with the first sentence referring to the individual view and the second sentence linking it to the information on health care. This is the best way to set out your answer.

3A. **(continued)**

Answer option 1: If you choose Graham Green

I most agree with the view of Graham Green for the following reasons.

Graham Green is correct to say he is concerned that a rich country like the USA does not provide health cover for so many of its citizens. This is supported by the fact that 36 million Americans have no health cover and 64% of Americans are either concerned or very concerned about this.

He is also correct to say that current government expense as a % of GDP is much greater than that of other countries. This is supported by the fact that 16% of the USA's GDP is spent on health with the next closest being France with 11% of its GDP.

He is correct to say that that the majority of the American public supports President Obama's health care plan. This is supported by the fact that support for the plan is over 50%.

These points clearly support my choice of Graham Green as the person I most agree with.

Reasons to reject Sarah Heart

I decided not to pick Sarah Heart because she is wrong to claim that the use of private insurance companies provides a perfectly good system of health care insurance for all American citizens. This is supported by the fact that 36 million Americans currently do not have any health cover at all.

She is also wrong to say the plan will cost the government money rather than saving it and that the estimated savings are low. This is supported by the fact that the plan will reduce government spending by an estimated 132 billion dollars over the first 10 years and as much as 1·3 trillion dollars during the following 10 years.

For these reasons I have rejected the view of Sarah Heart.

Answer option 2: If you choose Sarah Heart

I most agree with the view of Sarah Heart for the following reasons.

Sarah Heart correctly says that public opposition to the bill has been rising as more details emerge about the costs and disadvantages of the health plan. This is supported by the fact that opposition has risen from 46% in June to just under 50% in December.

She is also correct to say that doctors should be listened to and that many doctors are very unhappy with President Obama's health plan. This is supported by the fact that many doctors have left the American Medical Association over its support for the plan.

She correctly says that Americans who earn over $50,000 a year already contribute heavily in taxes to pay for health care for the poor and do not support the bill. This is supported by the fact that only 40% who earn over $50,000 a year are willing to pay higher taxes.

All of these points clearly support my choice of Sarah Heart as the person I most agree with.

Reasons to reject Graham Green

Graham Green is wrong to say that political opposition to the bill is not clear. This is supported by the fact that every Republican senator voted against the bill.

He is also wrong to say that everyone is willing to pay higher taxes in order to pay for health cover. This is supported by the fact that only 40% who earn over $50,000 are willing to pay higher taxes.

For these reasons I have rejected the view of Graham Green.

10 marks, Enquiry Skills

TOP EXAM TIP

In this type of question don't waste time trying to decide which option is the best. There is no right or wrong answer. There is always enough evidence to support either choice.

TOP EXAM TIP

Watch the time – you have just under 30 minutes in the Credit exam for each question area.

QUESTION 3B – CHINA

3B. (a)

HINT > In this section of the exam you should prepare for questions about the key concepts of **Ideology**, **Participation**, **Equality** and **Rights and Responsibilities**.

TOP EXAM TIP

Do not write your answers as lists or bullet points. Write in proper sentences.

The concept being assessed is **Equality**. You need to use understanding of the concept to provide detailed descriptions followed by detailed explanations with relevant examples. You should start by linking to the question.

Answers could include:

One economic inequality that exists is that some people have more money than others. This might be because they live in Special Economic zones, setting up their own business and keeping the profit they make for themselves. This has allowed people to be able to pay for a higher standard of living. People who do not live in Special Economic zones would not necessarily be able to do this.

If you live in a rural area you are more likely to be poorer than people who live in urban areas. This is because the government has focussed its economic growth in cities such as Shanghai and Beijing, who received an enormous amount of investment for the 2008 Olympic Games. People who live in rural areas still rely on agriculture for most of their income. Wages in agriculture are traditionally low. People who live in cities can earn a significant amount more than people who live in the countryside.

Inequalities exist in housing in China. Housing in rural areas is usually worse than in urban areas but there are also inequalities within urban areas. This is partly due to the huge number of migrant workers who have come to cities like Beijing to work. These migrant workers are often forced to live in hostel-type accommodation 'on-site'. There are very few amenities for them with very little living space. Workers in the cities who work in more skilled jobs can enjoy a better standard of accommodation.

Inequalities can also exist in education and at all levels of education. Getting good teachers in rural areas has proved challenging as wages can be low. Many people in rural areas stop their education after primary school, as there is no money available to advance further. Members of the Communist party have access to better educational opportunities than those people who are not members. This can lead to improved opportunities for entry to University courses for example.

8 marks, Knowledge and Understanding

TOP EXAM TIP

Remember you MUST use Chinese examples in your answers to get a good mark in this section.

(b)

Decision Making

In your answer, you need to make a clear choice.

To get full marks in this answer you again need to use all the information. Your answers must make explicit links between the background information about health care in China and Sources 1 and 2.

You are asked to choose who you most agree with. There is no right or wrong answer as the evidence supports both views. What matters is how you use the information to support your choice and how you reason your rejection of the other person.

You should clearly link your choice to the information about health care.

The following answers have been set out with the first sentence referring to the individual view and the second sentence linking it to the information on health care. This is the best way to set out your answer.

Answer option 1: If you choose Song Li

I most agree with the view of Song Li for the following reasons.

Song Li says that he is concerned that health reforms will not help people in rural parts of China.

In the information, Yan Yinlan, a village doctor, is also concerned about whether reforms will make a difference in rural areas.

Song Li thinks that the pharmaceutical companies will make the most money out of any reforms. The information suggests that this is an issue as in 2010 the companies are expected to make $25 billion and the information indicates that some drugs might become more expensive.

3B. **(continued)**

He continues to say that most of the 1,326 million people in China are already covered by health care insurance and the numbers covered are continuing to increase. This is supported by the information which shows that 1,133 million people were covered by health insurance in 2008, which is a huge improvement on 2004 when only 231 million were covered.

Furthermore he says that the Government is spending more on health. The information shows us the government is already spending more on health care. They spent about $150 billion in 2005 and about $250 billion in 2009.

All of these points clearly support my choice of Song Li as the person I most agree with.

I rejected Lin Yayang for the following reasons

- I decided not to pick Ms Lin as she is incorrect in saying that the government is not increasing spending on health care as this has clearly risen dramatically in the last five years.

- I also disagree with her when she says that the government has not made any changes to health care since the 1950s. The information tells us that the government reformed health care in the 1990s by switching to an insurance system.

For these reasons I have rejected the view of Lin Yayang.

Answer option 2: If you choose Lin Yayang

I most agree with the view of Lin Yayang for the following reasons.

Lin Yayang says that health care reforms in China have been very well thought out with many different groups involved in the consultation process. In the information it is clear that the Chinese Government has gone to a lot of effort to consult a wide range of individuals and groups on possible changes to health care. They have had expert teams looking at reform, outside agencies like WHO conducting independent research, and set up a website to get the views of the public.

Lin Yayang says that she, like many others in China, is very concerned about health care and wants to see improvements. This is supported by the fact that the information on health care tells us that there have been many complaints about things like medical fees in the current unpopular system and it tells us that doctors have welcomed the idea of reform.

She continues by saying that millions of Chinese do not have any health care cover. This is supported by the information as 400 million people are estimated to have no health cover according to the Ministry of Health.

Furthermore she says that people in China will also get better access to a wider range of medical drugs. This is also supported by the information which tells us that there will be a wider range of drug treatments as a result of changes.

All of these points clearly support my choice of Lin Yayang as the person I most agree with.

I rejected Song Li because

- I disagree with Mr Song when he says that health care reforms require a lot more consideration. The government has already consulted widely on the issue having meetings with pharmaceutical companies, experts and ordinary people.

- Although the pharmaceutical companies will benefit as Mr Song says, he is wrong to say that the people will not benefit. The information tells us that it will mean more money for the economy overall and more of a choice of drug treatments for people who are ill.

- Mr Song is correct to say that most people are covered by health insurance but clearly a large number are not, 400 million people, and they should not be forgotten about.

For these reasons I have rejected the view of Song Li.

10 marks, Enquiry Skills

TOP EXAM TIP

In this type of question don't waste time trying to decide which option is the best. There is no right or wrong answer. There is always enough evidence to support either choice.

TOP EXAM TIP

Watch the time – you have just under 30 minutes in the Credit exam for each question area.

SYLLABUS AREA 4 – INTERNATIONAL RELATIONS

TOP EXAM TIP

You don't need to do the whole exam paper in order. Look at the whole paper and start with the question area you think you will do best in. You should aim to keep question areas together, e.g. all of Area 3, then all of Area 1 and so on.

TOP EXAM TIP

In this section of the exam you should prepare for questions about the key concepts of **Need** and **Power**.

QUESTION 4

4.   (*a*)

 The Concept being assessed in this question is **Power**. You have to show understanding of the concept in your answer. You need to talk about the powers of the UN. Notice that the word 'power' is repeatedly used in the sample answer. Any three of the paragraphs below should be enough for full marks. You should open with a link to the question.

Link: The United Nations (UN) can do a number of things to promote peace.

Terrorism: The UN has agreements with other international organisations, such as the European Union, to share intelligence about terrorism and to ensure that no UN agencies are involved in the funding of terrorism directly or indirectly. UN members are increasingly coordinating their anti-terrorism measures. In 2006 all UN members agreed a Global Counter-Terrorism Strategy. This gives the UN and all its members more power to tackle terrorism effectively.

Sanctions: The UN can introduce economic sanctions. This means that they will tell all members not to trade with a certain group or country. This is often used in war situations like the conflict over Kosovo (sanctions were imposed on Serbia). Cutting off trade generally or specifically (e.g. blocking the supply of weapons) can be a very powerful tool for the UN. Economic sanctions have been used against Iraq and are currently in use against the terrorist group Al Qaeda.

Military action: The UN can only send in their peacekeeping troops once a ceasefire has been agreed. However they can support the actions of other groups. The UN has approved and supported the command of NATO over the International Security Assistance Force (ISAF) in Afghanistan. This allows the UN to exercise more power and influence in places with ongoing conflicts.

Peace talks and peacekeeping: The UN is involved in bringing different sides together in order to reach agreements. There have been ongoing peace talks between the Greeks and Turkish Cypriots over the future of the divided island. The UN has the power to bring these sides together but they can't make them agree. UN peacekeepers were sent to Cyprus in 1964 and they are still there in 2010. The peacekeeping force supervises the ceasefire and maintains a buffer zone between the two sides.

The UN in Kosovo: Kosovo became independent from Serbia in 2008 partly as a result of a UN peace plan. The UN had taken over the direct running of Kosovo in 1999. The UN Interim Administration Mission in Kosovo (UNMIK) then gradually reduced its governing role and paved the way for self-government and then independence. UNMIK continues to monitor the situation in Kosovo. This is an unusual example of the UN demonstrating a power by governing an area.

8 marks, Knowledge and Understanding

 HINT   Eight mark credit questions are sometimes split into two parts. If this happens in any of your questions make sure that you tackle both parts of the question or you will be marked down in the exam.

(*b*), (*c*), (*d*) and (*e*)

Investigating questions

Questions **4.** (*b*), (*c*), (*d*) and (*e*) below are an investigating set of questions.

Look out for the man with the question mark in his head – he shows you this is an investigating set of questions.

(*b*)

Hypothesis

 A hypothesis is a statement which can be proved or disproved.

You have to state a hypothesis relevant to the issue of "Terrorism and the UK."

To get full marks you need to show understanding of the issue.

4.   (continued)

The following would not be acceptable and would get no marks:
- What is terrorism?

- What are the main terrorist threats to the UK?

The following do not show much understanding and so would receive 1 mark only:
- Terrorism in the UK is a major concern.

- Terrorism is not a major issue in the UK.

The following hypothesis would receive 2 marks:
✓ Terrorist threats are now a major issue in Britain because of groups like Al Qaeda.

✓ Terrorist threats since September 2001 have led to increased security in Britain.

These are not the only possible options for this investigation area – see if you can come up with some more hypotheses of your own.

2 marks, Enquiry Skills

> **HINT**
>
> Your hypothesis must never be a question. If it has 'what', 'where', 'why', 'who', 'how' or 'when' then it is a question not a hypothesis.
>
> Don't use the exact wording of the boxed issue for the investigation. In the above examples 'terrorism' has been changed to 'terrorist threats.'

> **TOP EXAM TIP**
>
> Check carefully that your hypothesis is a statement and not a question.

(c)

> **Aims**
>
> Now you have to come up with aims that are relevant to your hypothesis.
>
> Your aims are what you would need to find out to prove or disprove your investigation hypothesis.
>
> You get one mark for each aim depending on how it relates to the hypothesis.

Hypothesis
"Terrorism is now a major issue in the UK because of new threats from groups like Al Qaeda."

Aims

✓ To find out about Al Qaeda terrorist attacks.

✓ To find out about public concerns about terrorism.

You may be able to think of some other aims. Try the other hypothesis and see if you can think of some aims to go with it.

2 marks, Enquiry Skills

> **TOP EXAM TIP**
>
> Check that your aims are related to your hypothesis.

(d)

> **Surveys**
>
> You need to think about what makes a good survey.
>
> You will get up to two marks for each point you make if it is well explained.
>
> Any two of the points below would be enough to get full marks.

Answers may include:

✓ The size of the sample – a survey asking the views of 10 000 people is likely to be more accurate than a survey only asking 10 people.

✓ Gender – to be an accurate reflection of everyone a good survey should have a fairly even split of male and female. Men and women may have different views on the issue.

✓ Age – similar to gender. People sometimes have different views on an issue depending on their age. A good survey should have a range of age groups covered if they want to reflect the views of everyone.

4.   (continued)

    ✓ Geographical spread – is the survey just covering one area? If it is only asking for the views of people in Glasgow then this is a limited area and it may not be an accurate reflection of how people across the UK feel about the issue.

    ✓ Sometimes a survey may be focused – this means that they only question a certain group because they only want to find out the views of young people, or another group, about the issue

Size, gender and age are the easiest issues to talk about in this answer. Other factors to consider are the type of questions (yes/no answers or multiple choice options), is the survey carried out over the phone, by post or as a face to face interview? All these tactics could impact on the results of the survey.

4 marks, Enquiry Skills

(e)

Use of Website

You need to show that you are aware of how to use a website effectively.

You will get one mark for saying what you would do and another for your explanation.

    ✓ To use the Home Office website for the investigation you could use the quick search box at the top right-hand side of the page. If key words from the investigation aims were typed in here it would search the website for related information.

    ✓ Depending on what your Hypothesis and aims are you could click on one of the subject area options on the left-hand side of the screen. Counter-terrorism would be the best option to pick from this list.

2 marks, Enquiry Skills

HINT

In this type of question you may be asked to state advantages or disadvantages of a range of methods. You will need to know the benefits and limitations of all common research methods. You will also need to understand how to use each method effectively. Methods include: interviews, Internet, surveys / questionnaires, letters, emails, libraries, newspapers, databases and observational visits.

TOP EXAM TIP

If you have time left you should check through your answers.